Scenes and Characters from Surtees (ed.)
From Algiers to Austria: The History of 78 Division
The Pageant of London
Merry England
Regiment of the Line: The Story of the Lancashire Fusiliers
Best Murder Stories (ed.)
The Gourmet's Companion (ed.)
Morton Shand's Books of French Wines (ed.)
In a Glass Lightly
The Compleat Imbiber (ed.)
Cognac
Lafite: The Story of Château Lafite-Rothschild
Bollinger: The Story of a Champagne
Mouton: The Story of Château Mouton-Rothschild
Wine with Food (with Elizabeth Ray)
The Wines of Italy
The Wines of France
The Wines of Germany

The Complete Book of Spirits and Liqueurs

Cyril Ray

MACMILLAN PUBLISHING CO., INC.
NEW YORK

Macmillan Publishing Co., Inc.
866 Third Avenue, New York, N.Y. 10022

Library of Congress Catalog Card Number: 78-58852

ISBN 0-02-601150-6

First American Edition 1978

Photography: Ed Suister
Cartography: Otto van Eersel
Illustrations: Annemieke Bunjes
Layout: Joop de Nijs gvn
Executive editor: Jaap Woudt
Picture research: Berty Bakker and Emma Hogan

Printed in the Netherlands by Drukkerij Meijer Wormerveer bv

Contents

In Place of an Introduction . . .

. . . each and every liqueur, in his opinion, corresponded in taste with the sound of a particular instrument. Dry curaçao, for instance, was like the clarinet with its piercing, velvety note; kümmel like the oboe with its sonorous, nasal timbre; crème de menthe and anisette like the flute, at once sweet and tart, soft and shrill. Then to complete the orchestra there was kirsch, blowing a wild trumpet blast; gin and whisky raising the roof of the mouth with the blare of their cornets and trombones; marc-brandy matching the tubas with its deafening din; while peals of thunder came from the cymbal and the bass drum, which arak and mastic were banging and beating with all their might.

He considered that this analogy could be pushed still further and that string quartets might play under the palatal arch, with the violin represented by an old brandy, choice and heady, biting and delicate; with the viola simulated by rum, which was stronger, heavier, and quieter; with vespetro as poignant, drawn-out, sad, and tender as a violoncello; and with the double-bass a fine old bitter, full-bodied, solid, and dark. One might even form a quintet, if this were thought desirable, by adding a fifth instrument, the harp, imitated to near perfection by the vibrant savour, the clear, sharp, silvery note of dry cumin.

The similarity did not end there, for the music of liqueurs had its own scheme of interrelated tones; thus, to quote only one example, Benedictine represents, so to speak, the minor key corresponding to the major key of those alcohols which wine-merchants' scores indicate by the name of green Chartreuse.

Once these principles had been established, and thanks to a series of erudite experiments, he had been able to perform upon his tongue silent melodies and mute funeral marches; to hear inside his mouth crème-de-menthe solos and rum-and-vespetro duets.

He even succeeded in transferring specific pieces of music to his palate, following the composer step by step, rendering his intentions, his effects, his shades of expression, by mixing or contrasting related liqueurs, by subtle approximations and cunning combinations.

At other times he would compose melodies of his own, executing pastorals with the sweet blackcurrant liqueur that filled his throat with the warbling song of a nightingale; or with the delicious cacaochouva that hummed sugary bergerets like the *Romances of Estelle* and the '*Ah! vous dirai-je, maman*' of olden days.

But tonight Des Esseintes had no wish to listen to the taste of music; he confined himself to removing one note from the keyboard of his organ, carrying off a tiny cup which he had filled with genuine Irish whiskey.

He settled down in his armchair again and slowly sipped this fermented spirit of oats and barley, a pungent odour of creosote spreading through his mouth.

J. K. Huysmans: *À Rebours* (1882)
(Robert Baldick's translation)

7

Distillation, the Heart of the Matter

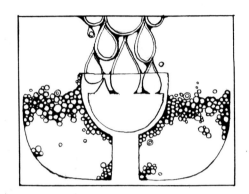

The spirits we discuss in this book – potable spirits – are produced by distillation.

Some, such as whisky and vodka, are marketed and imbibed pretty much – save in some cases for necessary mellowing by maturation – as they come from the still. But sweetened and flavoured cordials and liqueurs are also based upon such spirits. So distillation is the heart of the matter. It is the heart of the matter of this book, and it is also the technical means by which the heart, or the vital principle, of wine or grain or fruit or sugar-cane is isolated. It is the heart of the matter of drinks so different as the most tasteless of pre-prandial vodkas or aquavits and the sweetest and most luscious of after-dinner orange-flavoured liqueurs.

The word 'distillation' derives from the Latin verb *destillare,* which means to drop or to trickle down – an entirely logical derivation, for distillation is the process of turning a liquid into vapour by heating it, and then bringing it back to liquid form by condensation, in the course of which drops trickle down.

The simplest and most familiar example of distillation is the vaporising of surface water into clouds by the heat of the sun, and the subsequent condensation of the resultant vapour, by cooling, into rain, which drops or trickles down – unless it pours...

Different liquids boil, and thus become vapour, at different temperatures, and so by a simple extension of the basic principle of distillation the more volatile components of a mixed liquid can be vaporised, leaving the less volatile behind, and then be condensed and collected as a sort of quintessence of the original mixture.

The process was known to the ancients: the word *destillare* is used by a Roman writer of the first century A.D. in an account of the extraction of spirits of turpentine from resin, by boiling, and a Greek writer of the fifth century told how a sort of universal panacea could be distilled from a boiling mixture of sulphur, lime and water.

It is curious, though, that there is no reference in such classical writings as have come down to us to the distillation of alcohol from wine, though wine itself figures largely in Greek and Roman life and letters, and the possibility of its distillation is obvious: in wine there is both alcohol and water, and as alcohol becomes vapour at just over 78 degrees Centigrade, and water at a hundred, their separation is simple.

Wine is known to have been made by the fermentation of grape-juice in Neolithic times, ten thousand years ago and more, but is was long believed that the distillation from it of an alcoholic spirit had to wait until the alembic was devised by the Arabs, and that their secret reached the Western world by way of the Moors in Spain in the thirteenth century or thereabouts.

Recently, though, doubts have been cast upon these long-held beliefs: it has been pointed out that as the Arabs were taught by the Prophet to shun alcohol it is unlikely that they would trouble to produce it, and it has also been suggested that, even if they did so, they might well have made use of distilling techniques already devised either by Nestorian Christian alchemists of Byzantine times or, much earlier, by the Chinese.

Where all is speculation, this is as likely as any of the other suppositions – the Chinese have been credited with being first in the field with virtually everything else, from spaghetti to gunpowder, so why not the means by which we are vouchsafed our glass of schnapps or of cognac?

Our use of the Arabic-derived words 'alcohol' and 'alembic' is often brought forward as proof that the Arabs were the first to produce the one by means of the other. It is true that those western Europeans who took up alchemy received it from Arab masters, but it has been pointed out that what they took from

Medieval monasteries flavoured their medicinal distillations with herbs and spices. A monastery herb-garden, 1578.

A monastic pharmacy. Many of the herbs and spices used medicinally by monks and alchemists are still to be found in the commercial compounds of today.

Moorish books, using the Arabic words they found there for processes with as yet no names in European languages, the Moorish authors themselves may well have taken from Byzantine or Chinese forerunners.

Whoever the universal benefactors were, though, who first either stumbled upon or carefully devised the technique of producing ardent spirits, there is no doubt that by the thirteenth century such spirits were being distilled from wine in Spain, in Italy and in China – where it seems to have been achieved by freezing rather than by boiling (as applejack has been made in Canada at times, and the same sort of eau-de-vie in Calvados) and where some believed that, if imbibed, the resultant 'spirit and fluid secretion of wine will penetrate into a man's armpits and he will die'.

In which case, one wonders why the Chinese went to the trouble: we were wiser in the West, where the religious

houses flavoured with herbs and spices their distillations from wine and used them medicinally. It is said that the use of these new, alcoholically strong cordials spread widely throughout Europe during and after the Black Death (c. 1350). They may not have done much to cure that particularly vile and virulent form of typhus, but no doubt they helped to ease the sufferings by anaesthetizing the sufferers…

Much, if not all, of the drinking water of those days must have been contaminated: plagues and pestilences – probably the Black Death itself – must largely have been water-borne. So the art of distillation was applied to water itself by the knowledgeable and the cautious.

The distillation of spirits from the fermented product of grain may have come even earlier than the distillation of wine. Never mind whether Saint Patrick, as some pious Irish folk believe, not only

drove the snakes from Ireland, so that there is none there to this day, but also taught that country of saints and scholars to make potheen from a 'mash' of malted barley – it is certain, at any rate, that when, in the twelfth century, Strongbow and his Norman-English men-at-arms invaded that already (and still, alas) unhappy country, he found the distillation of whiskey from grain well-established.

A learned historian of Scotch whisky quotes a Scottish poet who held that the Irish invented and used it simply as an embrocation for their sick mules and that only his fellow-countrymen would ever have thought of drinking it.

However that may be, it was the Irish who taught the Scots how to make whisky, (the Scots, it must be noted, drop the 'e') and at about the same time such other northern peoples as the Scandinavians and the Balts, the Germans and the Dutch and the Poles, were making

their no doubt as yet pretty crude and primitive sorts of schnapps and vodkas.

One would not have thought that the French, who are far from the least quick-witted of peoples, would have lagged behind their Iberian neighbours to the south and their Hibernian neighbours to the north in the production of ardent spirits. But there seems to be no evidence that any sort of spirit was being distilled in France, whether from grain or from grape or any other fruit, before the fourteenth century.

It may be that the French were contented enough with their wines, already of outstandingly high quality compared with those of other countries, until the Italians, from whom they learned much of the arts of life, taught them to drink, to enjoy and, in consequence, to make distilled and flavoured liqueurs, and the Dutch, as will be shown later, encouraged them to make the greatest of all brandies.

When they did come to distilling spirits, whether from wine or from wild fruits, the French called them *eaux de vie*, waters of life, as the Romans had called them *aquae vitae*, which survives, almost unchanged from the Latin, in Scandinavian languages. And the word 'whisky' (or, as in Ireland and the United States, 'whiskey') is an anglicisation of the Gaelic *uisge beatha*, which means precisely and literally the same thing. Certainly, all the distilled spirits – waters of life – and their derivatives, used with discretion can be, as Bernard Berenson used to say of great paintings, *life-enhancing*, which is why I write about them here.

Virtually all spirits these days reach the consumer much weaker, alcoholically, than when they leave the still. Some are so fully distilled and rectified as to become more or less neutral or 'silent' spirit, subsequently flavoured, more – as with gin; or less – as with vodka.

Some, such as the various brandies and whiskies, are so much less fully distilled and rectified as to retain a great deal of the character and flavour of the liquors they derive from, whether these in their turn derive from grape or from grain. Some neutral spirits, as we shall see, are used merely as bases for rich, sweet cordials – in most cases, though not all, their alcoholic content much reduced by the addition of syrups and the essences of herbs or fruits.

The others, though, that we have mentioned – the spirits that are drunk for their own sake, such as rum, gin, whisky, brandy and the like – are made potable by the addition of distilled water, to varying extents, lest their strength should overwhelm their flavours (or their imbibers).

The governments of pretty well all countries in which wines and spirits are at all widely sold exact duty on them at rates determined by their alcoholic content – another reason for regulating this at the point of production. This is achieved by the addition of distilled water – distillation, this time, for the sake of purity.

In the United States and the United Kingdom (and in most countries that were or are still members of the British Commonwealth) alcoholic strength is expressed as being so much under or over 'proof'.

The word dates from a time less precisely scientific than ours when, in 1816, Bartholomew Sikes devised a new method of determining alcoholic content. If, after salination with a mixture of alcohol and water, gunpowder burned when ignited, this was 'proof', by the Sikes method, of a specific amount of alcohol.

With more accurate means of mensuration, it was found that Sikes's 'proof' – the minimum alcoholic strength necessary – was 57.10 per cent by volume. This was 100 per cent 'proof' or 'Sikes'.

A sixteenth-century distillery.
From Hieronymus Braunschweig's 'Das Buch zu destillieren', 1519.

Right: 'The contented drinker' a painting by Adriaan van Ostade (1610–1685).

12

By some curiously tacit consensus of international opinion this has been deemed unacceptably high for normal drinking, and in Britain, for instance, most brands of whisky, gin and other spirits are sold at 70 degrees of proof, which is to say 30 degrees under proof – but it is the 70 degrees that figures on the labels.

Although both the United States and the United Kingdom use 'proof' as a measure, they determine it differently, so that with the spirit to be measured at 16 degrees Centigrade, proof spirit in Britain is 57.10 per cent of pure alcohol by volume, whereas in the United States it is exactly 50. Thus it is that standard brands of blended Scotch whisky are labelled correctly for the British market at 70 degrees of proof, and for the American at 80 degrees.

Measures differ yet again in European countries: in France and Italy, for instance, the alcoholic content of spirits and liqueurs is stated in terms of degrees Gay-Lussac, which is to say as a percentage of the volume, in Germany as a percentage of weight. The equivalent on a French label of 70 degrees on a British and 80 on an American would be 40 degrees.

The sweet fruit liqueurs are usually much weaker than whiskies, brandies, gins and the like; so are most of the herb and citrus fruit liqueurs, but these do vary, and some few are uncommonly high in alcohol, as we shall see later. So are some few vodkas. But the thirsty traveller can be reasonably sure that from Naples to New York, Rome to Rotterdam and Reykjavik, the most widely advertised, best known, and reliable brands of whisky, gin, brandy, rum and vodka will be, in British, French and American terms respectively, a familiar and fairly safe 70; 40; 80 – vital statistics in a sense or, at any rate, aqua-vital...

A modern distillery – that of the Bordeaux firm of Marie Brizard.

Right: From Naples to New York, Rome to Rotterdam, well-known brands woo their hoped-for customers with colour – and sometimes with wit.

2

A History of flavoured Liqueurs

When we linger after dinner over such pretty little liquid sweetmeats as cherry brandy or Green Chartreuse, crème de menthe or Cordial Médoc, their colours twinkling and gleaming like fragments of stained glass, we are indebted to medieval monks, to the high-Renaissance Italy of the Medicis, and to the seventeenth-century courtiers of Versailles.

Long before western Europe first took to distillation, which was probably in the twelfth century, and then to the production of brandies and whiskies, the wines of the Middle Ages, many of which must have been thin and sour – the arts of viticulture and of vinification, and the merits of maturation being imperfectly understood – were made palatable with herbs and spices, honey and flower-petals. Much of this dressing-up of wine was done by the housewife in her kitchen, but much, too, by alchemists in their attics and monks in their monasteries, as magic potions and as medicines. For with spices and sweetening and seasonings wine could be made, or could be made to seem, health-restoring or passion-arousing: it must be that something was understood, however unscientifically, about the aphrodisiac effect of certain hot and irritant spices, if we are to account for the frequent mention, throughout medieval literature, of love-potions and their effects.

(The legend of Tristan and Isolde is not only an imperishable love-story; perhaps it should be a footnote to the history of wine and food as well.)

It was only long after the art of distillation became generally known that it was learned that the spirits thus produced became palatable only after maturing in wood.

All the same, men and women wanted to drink the raw rasping stuff for the warmth it gave to the cockles of the heart, for the alcoholic kick – or alcoholic amnesia – or for courage, whether on battlefield or in bedroom.

Many, though, must have screwed up their faces, or held their noses, as they tossed down the colourless, fiery liquid and wondered whether it could not be made more agreeable to nose and to palate – perhaps even to the eye.

The clue lay in what mistresses of the house, magicians and men of God had long been doing with varying degrees of skill and success to the wines of the time by the addition of herbs and sweetening, colouring matter, scents and spices. The newly-discovered spirits as a base for these flavoured cordials were more stable than wine, and lent themselves more readily to experiment, for a spiced and flavoured brandy would keep, as wine would not, to be tasted later against a different recipe.

It is generally supposed that it was Catherine de' Medici who introduced sweetened and flavoured liqueurs of this sort into France when she arrived from Florence in 1533 to marry the Dauphin, later to become Henri II.

one authority – William Younger, in his scholarly *Gods, Men and Wine,* – maintains that such were being imported into France as early as the 14th century. It is likely enough that monks were gathering fragrant herbs in the Normandy meadows at the same time as their brothers in God were similarly busy in the hills of northern Italy, and for similar reasons.

The importance of Catherine's place in social history does not depend on whether or not she was the first to bring sweet liqueurs from Italy into France, but on her establishing a courtly taste and thus, in time, a general fashion for them.

Alchemists at work. A German picture from the early seventeenth century.

Right: Dutch sailors of the seventeenth century brought oranges home from Curaçao in the West Indies and Curaçao liqueur, made from the same kind of oranges to this day, is still world-famous.'

In apparent contradiction to this, the French firm that now makes Bénédictine claims that its liqueur was first compounded by the monk Dom Bernard Vincelli in about 1510.

One learns to be sceptical, though, about the dates given in commercial brochures, and even if the claim is well-founded, it does not detract from Catherine de' Medici's importance in the history of western European manners and customs.

I have written elsewhere that 'It is a commonplace to historians of ideas … that at any one time there will be men of an enquiring turn of mind, widely separated from each other in space, in language, in culture and in technical resources, working unknown to each other on the same problems.'

We know that sweet liqueurs were already being made in Venice and Turin, as well as in Catherine's native Tuscany;

She arrived not only with the first *commedia dell'arte* company to be seen in France, but with a complete kitchen staff, bringing with them such Italian vegetables, hitherto unknown in France, as artichokes, broccoli and savoy cabbages, as well as the most elaborate confections of sugar and pastry and marzipan and preserved fruits.

What more likely than that Florentine liqueurs were served after the Florentine cooks' delicious and, to the French, new-fangled Italian dishes, served in the new-fangled Italian way and eaten with the equally new-fangled forks?

And it was a year after Catherine's wedding that her father-in-law, Francis I, is said to have tasted the native French Bénédictine, and found it good.

This was still, in the words of the old English chronicler, the age of 'the discoverie of Cathay and divers other regions, dominions, islands and places unknown', and levy was made upon the spices of the Eastern and the citrus fruits of the Western world to augment the herbs of Western Europe as enrichments, enliveners and preservers of distilled spirits.

Dried ginger was known to the ancient Romans, but by the middle of the sixteenth century Spanish ships were bringing the fresh roots from the West Indies, already yielding their oranges to the distilleries of the Netherlands.

The seventeenth century saw fruits, herbs and spices, hitherto unknown, being brought from the West Indies – a map of 1740.

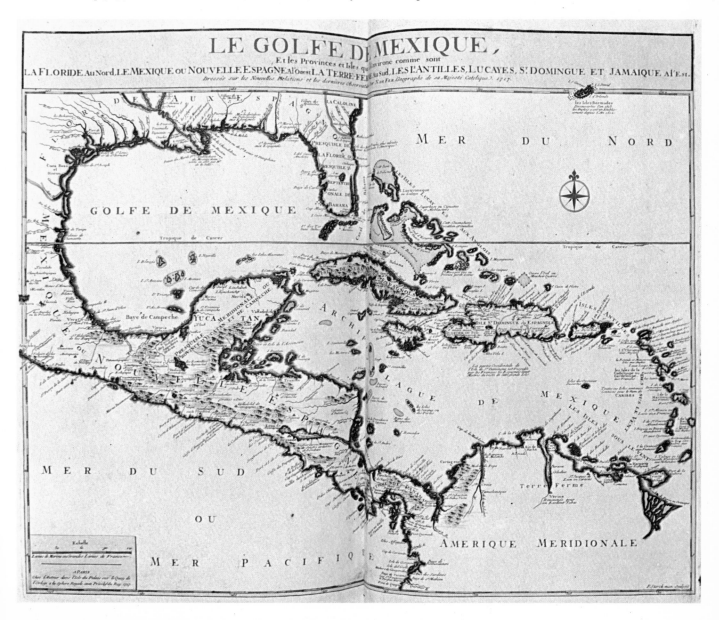

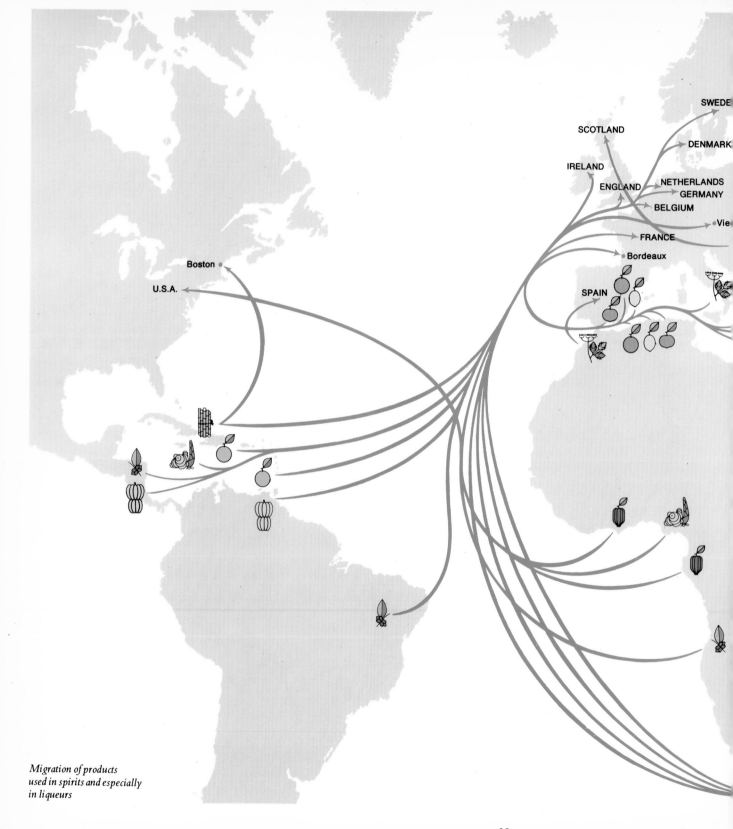

SWEDE
SCOTLAND
DENMARK
IRELAND
NETHERLANDS
ENGLAND
GERMANY
BELGIUM
Vie
FRANCE
Boston
Bordeaux
U.S.A.
SPAIN

*Migration of products
used in spirits and especially
in liqueurs*

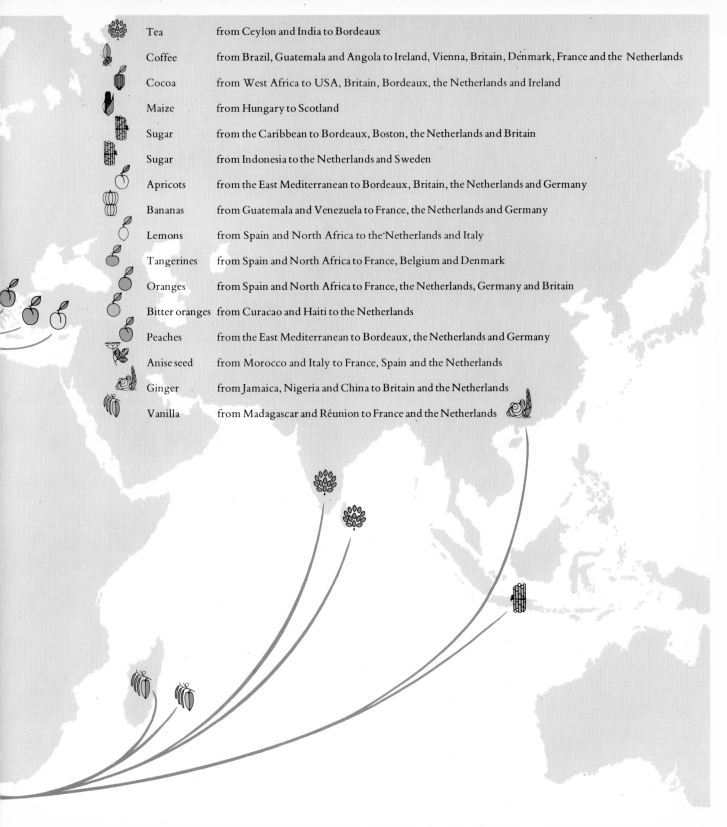

Tea	from Ceylon and India to Bordeaux
Coffee	from Brazil, Guatemala and Angola to Ireland, Vienna, Britain, Denmark, France and the Netherlands
Cocoa	from West Africa to USA, Britain, Bordeaux, the Netherlands and Ireland
Maize	from Hungary to Scotland
Sugar	from the Caribbean to Bordeaux, Boston, the Netherlands and Britain
Sugar	from Indonesia to the Netherlands and Sweden
Apricots	from the East Mediterranean to Bordeaux, Britain, the Netherlands and Germany
Bananas	from Guatemala and Venezuela to France, the Netherlands and Germany
Lemons	from Spain and North Africa to the Netherlands and Italy
Tangerines	from Spain and North Africa to France, Belgium and Denmark
Oranges	from Spain and North Africa to France, the Netherlands, Germany and Britain
Bitter oranges	from Curacao and Haiti to the Netherlands
Peaches	from the East Mediterranean to Bordeaux, the Netherlands and Germany
Anise seed	from Morocco and Italy to France, Spain and the Netherlands
Ginger	from Jamaica, Nigeria and China to Britain and the Netherlands
Vanilla	from Madagascar and Réunion to France and the Netherlands

For the same century that saw Catherine de Medici's guests fiddling with their forks, and Francis's being proffered his Bénédictine, the oldest Dutch distilling firm still in existence, Bols, was founded, probably in 1575 or thereabouts. And we know that firms were founded there earlier still that have not survived. It is significant that Bols was making flavoured sweet liqueurs from the beginning: anisette was the first, probably from the anise-seed of the Levant, but Curaçao, from the oranges of the Dutch West Indies, was probably not far behind. Of the more traditional herb liqueurs, the original Chartreuse recipe – much modified in later years – was given by one of Henri IV's marshals to a Carthusian monastery in 1605 and, later in the century, Louis XIV's physician soothed the monarch's agonies of indigestion – Le Roi Soleil was the grossest of guzzlers – with a post-prandial cordial compounded of aniseed, fennel, dill, coriander, caraway, camomile and sugar, all in spirit.

In 1676 this liqueur was allowed to be sold to the general public, by street vendors, along with other sweetened spirits. The French to this day refer to sweet after-dinner drinks as 'digestifs': the line of descent from Louis XIV's stomach-comforters is clear. For although, throughout the eighteenth-century, brandy in particular, and spirits in general, became steadily more palatable, as the virtues of blending and of maturation became more fully

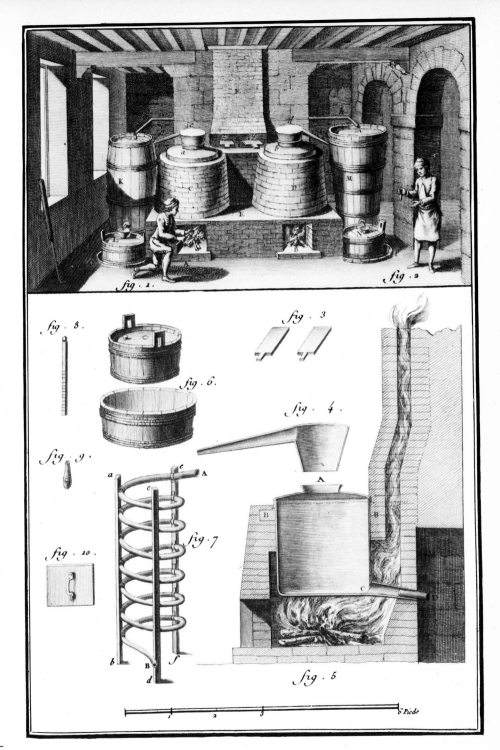

Distillateur
d'Eau-de-Vie.

Monks distilling spirits and steeping herbs for flavouring.

The old monastic and the new lay distilleries vied with each other in compounding liqueurs from secret recipes as individual specialities of their houses. When the young Italian Justerini came to London from Bologna in 1749, to set up the house that still flourishes as Justerini and Brooks, he brought with him recipes for an orange brandy and an Aqua Mirabilis, and at almost the same time, in 1755, Marie Brizard – a name still famous in the world of liqueurs – set up business in Bordeaux, armed with a recipe for anisette given to her by a West Indian she had tended during an epidemic that had swept the city.

Innocent-sounding names, those anisettes and orange brandies and Signor Justerini's Aqua Mirabilis, compared with some that have been recorded as offered for sale in eighteenth-century England and France – Eau Nuptiale, Belle de Nuit, Huile de Cythère and Huile de Vénus; and with the down-to-earth Dutch, cozened by

understood, a taste for the flavoured liqueurs remained in men's – perhaps even more especially in women's – gastronomic memories.

So they continued to be produced, many of them in monasteries – as one of the noblest and best-known still is – for monks by long tradition were cultivators of herbs, skilled in medicine, and practised in the art of spicing wine.

More and more commercial firms, though, now set themselves up after the fashion of Bols and its Dutch contemporaries.

The oldest surviving French firm, Rocher Frères, was founded in 1705 at La Côte St. André, in the Alpine foothills of the Dauphiné – brigand country in those days, but rich in herbs for the distillers of liqueurs, as the great Chartreuse establishment also bears witness, at Voiron, only a dozen miles away, and as the delicate vermouths of Chambéry still remind us.

24

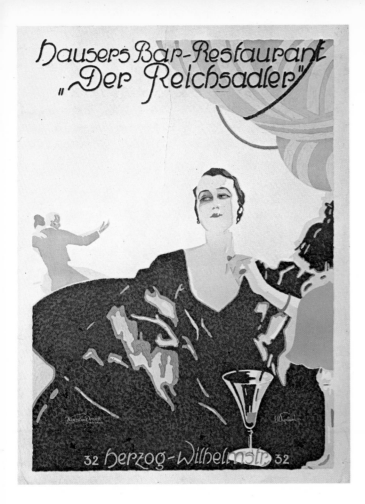

The cocktail craze was floated upon the mixed-up drinks of the mixed-up nineteen-twenties, and ladies looked naughty or looked mischievous when pressed to take a Between the Sheets or a Bosom Caresser.

such concoctions as Hoe Langer Hoe Liever – The Longer the Better – and Hempje Ligt Op, which is to say 'Up with your shirt', both of which are still to be found in Bols's list.

It is clear that not every purchaser of the liqueurs of the eighteenth century was primarily concerned with his digestion, and as this was the Age of Reason they would be regarded, hopefully, as aphrodisiacs rather than referred to with superstitious awe, in the medieval manner, as love philtres.

There was to be no such titillation again in the nomenclature of short drinks until the cocktail craze of the nineteen-twenties, when candy was dandy but liquor was quicker – or so they hoped – with their Between the Sheets, their Monkey Gland, and their Bosom Caresser.

Curiously enough, the aphrodisiac aura of some of those liqueurs of the eighteenth century has lingered longer than the more feverishly-named mixed-up drinks of the mixed-up twentieth century. The Bosom Caresser and the Monkey Gland have disappeared from the cocktail bar, almost certainly for ever, but still amongst the liqueurs being commercially produced, and listed in this book, are Parfait Amour and Forbidden Fruit.

Long may they flourish, and the hopes we build upon them . . .

Grape Brandies

3

From as far north as the Rhine valley to as far south as Australia's Hunter River, from Soviet Georgia to California, every country that grows wine also makes brandy, for brandy is simply a distillate of wine. Nothing could be simpler. I have drunk good, bad and indifferent brandies in South Africa and in Cyprus, in Israel and in Italy, and a perfectly horrible brandy in Iran called Grande Champagne Cognac Impériale, made by a company called Ararat Limited, and smelling of chocolate creams.

I have drunk bad brandy even in France, though that is the country that produces the most famous brandy in the world – cognac – and then, as though that were not enough, the second most famous – armagnac.

The differences in style between one good brandy and another good brandy, and the difference in quality between good, bad, indifferent and perfectly horrible brandies derive from methods of distillation, from the methods and the duration of the maturing process, from the wood in which the brandy is matured (if at all) and from what colouring, softening, sweetening and flavouring matters are added before bottling.

I recall that at one of Israel's wineries, for instance, some years ago, I must have pulled a face, hard though I was trying to be the courteous guest, over the commercial brandies that I was being shown, one after another – far too dark, far too sweet, far too artificially flavoured – because eventually the director said,

'I think perhaps you'd prefer a brandy I distil just for myself and a few friends: it was put into cask a dozen years ago, and I've done absolutely nothing to it since. No caramel, no sugar, no flavouring – just brandy, matured in oak.' Very good it was, too.

And although in the two years, 1950–52, that I spent as a newspaper correspondent in Moscow, I was never able to lay lip on a decent glass of brandy, though I tried hard, even in such temples of the Soviet belly as the Aragvi Restaurant, upon which Stalin himself was said to look kindly, yet a really fine old Georgian brandy was produced at our hotel in Kiev where I stayed as one of the press party that accompanied Mr. Macmillan on his official visit to Mr. Khrushchev in 1959. Nor can the difference be attributed to the change in the Soviet regime: the brandies I had tasted in Moscow had been far too heavily softened, sweetened and coloured.

It must be admitted that even cognac, the greatest of all brandies, is permitted by French law – stringent as it is in its control of methods of production and of nomenclature of wines, spirits and foodstuffs – the addition of distilled water, to bring the spirit down to an acceptable alcoholic strength (70 degrees proof on the Sikes scale for the British market, which is virtually the same as the French 40 Gay-Lussac, and the American 80) and strictly limited admixtures of cane-sugar and of caramel.

Vineyards in the Charentes – birthplace of the eau de vie de vin which the world knows as cognac.

The sugar is to soften the asperities still to be found in young or youngish brandies; it may be added directly, or it may be added in the form of a syrup, dissolved in brandy, but in this case the brandy in which it is dissolved must itself be entitled to the appellation 'cognac'. The amount added is limited by law to two per cent by volume.

So is the amount of caramel, which is burnt sugar. This is not to sweeten the blend – I am told that it is tasteless – but to deepen the colour of a commercial blend, and then keep it consistent, year after year. Although there is a fashion in some quarters for lighter and drier brandies (and rums and whiskies) this is not widespread. On the whole, brandy-consumers take a deep colour to mean age and quality – or so the shippers believe. In any case, they expect their favourite brand to be always the same shade, whenever and wherever they drink it: caramel ensures this. The amount of

28

caramel used is also restricted by law: again some two per cent by volume. What is not restricted by law is the addition of an infusion of oak-chips *(le boisé)*, for this limits itself. It is meant to give the effects of extra age to a blend, the argument being that if it is contact with the wood of the cask that mellows a brandy, then the addition of an infusion of the same sort of wood will hasten the process.

But it is not only contact with wood that matures a brandy: it is the breathing through the pores of the wood – breathing alcohol out and oxygen in. So although the addition of an infusion of oak-chips will give the colour and the tannin, it will not give the softness, and this is why it must be used sparingly. Too much will merely make the brandy darker and woodier (which is what happens to brandies left too long in cask) but without the true mellowness of age. For it is maturing in oak that gives cognac much of its character and its quality – along, of course, with type of grape, soil, climate and blending.

First, though, it must be understood that it is distilled differently from other spirits – from grain whisky, from gin and vodka, from California brandy, (which is distilled like grain whisky), and even from French 'grape-brandies', so-called, which is to say brandies made in France, but not entitled to be called cognac or armagnac, and also from armagnac, its only rival in fame and in finesse, but dissimilar in making and in style.

Cognac is the product, as it always has been, and as French law insists, of pot stills – not of the patent stills in which gin, grain whisky and vodka are produced. Basically, the principle of distillation is simple, as has been made clear in chapter 1.

The difference between distillation by pot still and distillation by patent still, put very briefly, is this:
By a continuous distillation process, the patent still rectifies the alcohol as it is being separated from the water in whatever the original fermented liquid may be, thus producing a strong, comparatively pure, or neutral, spirit. Such a spirit retains very little of those secondary characteristics of the original liquid that give flavour, and this is why the patent-still, or continuous, method is used to produce gin, which requires to have its flavours added after distillation, and vodka, the virtue of which is precisely its tastelessness and lack of aroma.

Cognac is and has always been the product of pot stills. A modern distillery in Cognac.

(This, too, as will be seen in the following chapter, is why the Scotch whisky of commerce is a blend of grain whisky, produced by the patent still process, to give lightness and dryness, but not much flavour or fragrance, and the flavoury, fragrant, heavier malt, produced by pot still.)

The pot still, on the other hand, with the two separate, non-continuous, distillations required both by tradition

An Armagnac distillery. Armagnac is distilled only once, cognac twice : hence, cognac has the more delicate, armagnac the earthier flavour.

Pot still

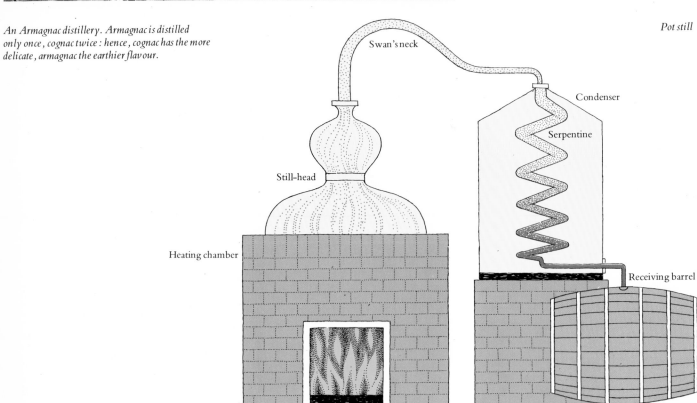

Swan's neck

Condenser

Serpentine

Still-head

Heating chamber

Receiving barrel

and by law, is slow in use, and thus can easily be controlled, so that unwanted elements can be rejected, others put back for further distillation, but much of the character of the original liquid retained. One of the major informing differences between cognac and armagnac, the other French brandy of distinction, is that whereas armagnac is also produced in old-fashioned pot stills, it is distilled only once, to cognac's twice, but at a lower temperature. Cognac leaves the still with an average strength of seventy per cent of alcohol, leaving thirty per cent for the congenerics or 'impurities' that are the flavoury characteristics of the finished product; armagnac leaves the still with an average alcoholic strength of fifty per cent, leaving even more room than cognac for congenerics. Cognac is thus more delicate; armagnac retains even more of the character of the earth in which the grapes grew, of the grapes themselves and thus of the wine from which the brandy was distilled: it is racier of the soil.

And the soil is different from that which is the birthplace of cognac. The climate is different, too – armagnac comes from farther south: the grape ripens under a hotter sun.

The only important factor common to both is the main species of grape that produces the wine from which cognac and armagnac are distilled.

Cognac matures slowly in the golden casks of Tronçais or Limousin oak.

Patent still or Coffey still

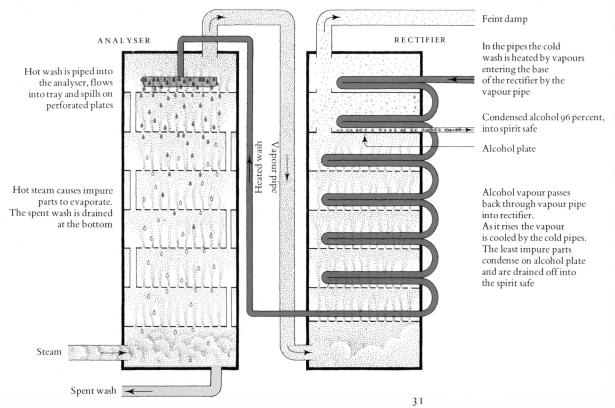

ANALYSER

Hot wash is piped into the analyser, flows into tray and spills on perforated plates

Hot steam causes impure parts to evaporate. The spent wash is drained at the bottom

Heated wash

Vapour pipe

Steam

Spent wash

RECTIFIER

Feint damp

In the pipes the cold wash is heated by vapours entering the base of the rectifier by the vapour pipe

Condensed alcohol 96 percent, into spirit safe

Alcohol plate

Alcohol vapour passes back through vapour pipe into rectifier. As it rises the vapour is cooled by the cold pipes. The least impure parts condense on alcohol plate and are drained off into the spirit safe

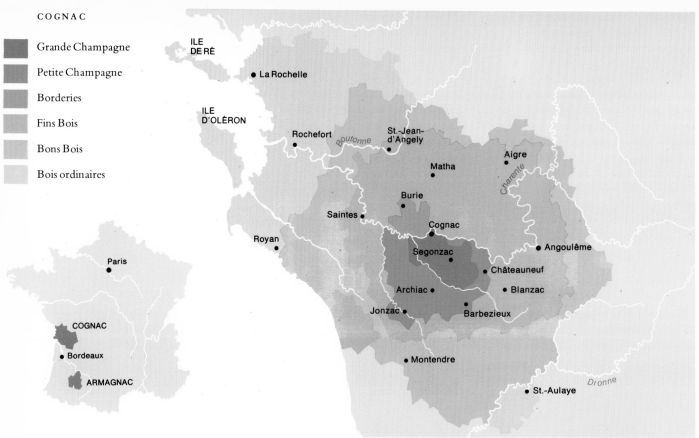

ILE
DE RÉ

ILE
D'OLÉRON

La Rochelle

Rochefort

St.-Jean-
d'Angely

Matha

Aigre

Burie

Saintes

Cognac

Segonzac

Angoulême

Châteauneuf

Royan

Paris

Archiac

Blanzac

COGNAC

Jonzac

Barbezieux

Bordeaux

ARMAGNAC

Montendre

St.-Aulaye

Dronne

Charente

Boutonne

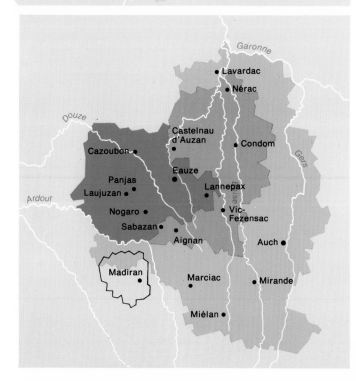

Garonne

Lavardac

Nérac

Douze

Castelnau
d'Auzan

Condom

Cazoubon

Eauze

Panjas

Lannepax

Laujuzan

Ardour

Vic-
Fezensac

Nogaro

Sabazan

Auch

Aignan

Madiran

Marciac

Mirande

Miélan

Gers

The earthier character of armagnac is emphasised by its being matured in vats of the local black oak, seamed with black veins and mottled with black knots, which brings the brandy on more quickly than cognac, giving it its darker colour and a heavier flavour, whereas cognac matures more slowly in the lighter, golden oak of the more northerly Limousin or Tronçais forests. No other oak is used for cognac.

Just as the region from which cognac may be produced if it is to be described as cognac is strictly defined by law (as are the type of grape, the method of pruning, the still and the distillation) so, too, are the zones within the region.

These lie in more or less concentric circles, as follows:

Grande Champagne
Petite Champagne
Borderies
Fins Bois
Bons Bois
Bois ordinaires

The names of the districts Grande and Petite Champagne have nothing to do with that part of France, three or four hundred miles to the north-east, whence comes the sparkling wine that is as much the paragon of its own kind as is cognac among brandies. It means simply 'open country', whereas the Bois brandies – 'fins', 'bons' and 'ordinaires' – come from country that was once thickly wooded. The list is in descending order of importance and of price commanded. The difference between Grande and Petite Champagne is so small that the two zones are bracketed together in defining the appellation 'Fine Champagne'. For a cognac to be so-called it must consist of brandies only from these two zones and of at least fifty per cent Grande Champagne.

Some houses, such as Rémy-Martin, pride themselves on producing only Fine Champagne blends, but others, such as

Hennessy and Martell, hold firmly that better-balanced cognacs are produced by skilful blending of the two Champagne qualities with the quicker-maturing, fuller-flavoured, Borderies and Fins Bois. Other firms still, such as Delamain, which produces a notable 'Pale and Dry', maintain a characteristic style partly by methods of blending, partly by maturing for long periods for the sake of mellowness, but in especially big casks of much-used oak, so that less than is usual

elsewhere of the colour and the tannin of wood is absorbed by the ageing spirit. Each house, then, has its own character: within each house – most, at any rate – quality depends largely on age, and the definition of this too is controlled by French law.

Three-star brandies must be more than one year old: in practice they are usually at least three. (Throughout the code, the age given is that of the youngest brandy in a blend.)

The next older quality is usually styled VSOP, in which case it must be at least four years old – in practice, usually much more. Some firms are adopting brand-names of their own – Martell's and Hennessy's VSOP qualities are called 'Medaillon' and 'Bras d'Or', respectively.

It is a measure of the historic importance in the cognac trade of the English-speaking peoples that VSOP stands for 'Very Superior Old Pale',

though Rémy-Martin, who do not produce a three-star, but specialise in VSOP, have patented the old French jest that it stands for 'versez sans oublier personne' – 'pour it out without forgetting anyone' – while Alec Waugh, the novelist, claims to have been told in Cognac itself that it stands for 'vieux, sans opinion politique'.

In the highest category, which requires nothing more than a minimum of five

'Napoleon', 'Cordon Bleu', 'Extra Vieille' etc. are the honorifics the well-known houses give to their superior qualities.

years old, come not only such honorifics as Extra, Extra Vieille, Vieille Réserve, Très Vieille Grande Réserve, Cordon Bleu, and Cordon Argent, but even Napoléon, and Grande Réserve de l'Empereur.

For there is no such thing as 'Napoleon' brandy: generally speaking, brandy does not improve in wood after about fifty years (varying a little according to the climate in which it is kept and to the youth or age of the wood) and not at all in bottle. A 1900 cognac bottled in 1930 is still a thirty-year old in 1977.

Most of the old bottles labelled as 'Napoleon' brandy are either blends bottled before the last war and given the date of the oldest brandy in the blend, which might well be only a few drops (this practice is now illegal) or from a range that was put up in Cognac during the first decade of this century for the Paris luxury trade.

Other wine-growing regions of France produce brandy – *eau de vie de vin*, or labelled in the United Kingdom and the United States as 'French grape brandy' to distinguish it from cognac and armagnac. In France, it may be called '*fine*', and there is a particularly good fine de la Marne, from the champagne district. Generally speaking, cognac sets the pattern, and the better the grape brandy the nearer to cognac in style, though it is usually less subtle in its nuances of flavour.

35

The eau de vie distilled from the compressed cake of skins, stalks and pips of the grapes after wine-making is known as 'marc' in France, 'grappa' in Italy and 'Trester' in Germany.

As well as such eaux de vie de vin as cognac, armagnac and the other grape-brandies of France, an eau de vie is distilled from the solid matter left in the presses after the juice has been extracted for fermenting into wine. The compressed cake of skins, stalks and pips is known as 'marc', and 'eau de vie de marc' is usually known as 'marc' simply.

In Italy and in California, precisely the same spirit is known as 'grappa' and in Germany it is 'tresterschnapps'. Usually, these spirits are coarse and fiery, but they can be refined and aged to greater delicacy, still retaining, though, the woody or strawlike or earthy taste which is what commends them to their devotees. Of the French marcs, those of Burgundy and of Champagne are especially esteemed, and of the marcs of Burgundy, that of Meursault is much admired, as is the marc de Gewürztraminer of Alsace. In Italy there are old grappas, matured in

Wherever wine is available, eau de vie de vin, brandy or Branntwein can be distilled. 'Der Brandtewein' a German picture by M. Engelbrecht.

oak, that have some merit, and grappa alla ruta is delicately tinted and flavoured by a grass-like herb, in much the same way as the Polish vodka, Zubrowka, mentioned in chapter 5.

Italy produces brandy, too – virtually all of it from big commercial concerns such as Stock and Buton. Both pot stills and patent stills are used for distilling: the brandy for sale is a blend, as is Scotch whisky, and usually sweetened and even, perhaps, flavoured.

Italian wine goes to Germany to be made into brandy, as does wine from the south of France and Yugoslavia: German wine cannot be spared for distillation. Production is almost entirely in the hands of the firm of Asbach. As in Cognac, distillation is by pot still and maturation in Limousin oak, but this is not to say that a cognac quality or even style is achieved: German brandy is light, sweetish and unsubtle in comparison.

The best-known Spanish brandy, Fundador, is heavier and coarser, but there are others that are more highly regarded, and those of Catalonia, with the firm of Torres outstanding, are said to resemble good armagnacs – the regions are not far apart. Portuguese brandy, aguardiente, is not so well-known abroad as that of Spain. It is drier, but it is not in the cognac class.

Greece and Turkey both produce brandies, and name them cognac (or kanyak), what's more, a practice forbidden to, or forsworn by the Western

world – those countries, that is, that respect or have been obliged by their own legal processes to respect the French law of appellation.

They vary in quality, but the best Greek brandies are not without merit. Mastika, or masticha, is resinated Greek brandy, and ouzo (see chapter 5) the anise-flavoured, pastis-like aperitif, has a brandy base.

I have referred already to Israeli brandy, the commercial varieties of which do not commend themselves to cultivated tastes. Cyprus, on the other hand, produces what is probably the Eastern Mediterranean's nearest approach to cognac in style, thanks to the years of British influence on the island. What is not British, though is the habit of the islanders of drinking one version or another of brandy sour, which is virtually the national drink (the Greek-Cypriot national drink, that is: Turks are Moslems, and some of them even observant Moslems).

I write 'one version or another' for where three or four Cypriots are gathered together there are four or five different recipes – it is only generally agreed that there should be two parts of brandy to one of bottled lemon squash, a dash or so of bitters, ice, a slice of lemon, the lot made into a longish drink with soda water.

Some add sugar, which I think unnecessary with bottled squash; some crust the rim of the glass with sugar, which I consider to be at once pretentious and uncomfortable; some add a bright red 'cocktail' cherry, and it shall not be forgiven them.

Half the world away, most Latin-Americans (and many North-Americans) drink pisco sour, based on the spirit produced everywhere in South America that the grape grows, sometimes distilled in the same way as any grape brandy, from wine, sometimes from the residual solids after winemaking, in the same way as marc and grappa. It is as well, in those parts, to enquire.

South Africa is a country that grows wine but drinks brandy and, indeed, brandy has been distilled in South Africa since 1672 – within a mere seven years of the first vines' being planted in the Cape. Today, the standard is high, largely because of government control which ensures, among other factors affecting quality, that only suitable wine is distilled, that 25 per cent of every blend must be pot still brandy, and that there must be at least three years of maturation in oak. Rebates for longer ageing make for very good premium qualities.

Australia is another wine-growing country where government control over the production of brandy ensures a consistently high standard.

One of the world's greatest brandy-producing regions is California, the output of which is more than that of France – cognac, armagnac, grape-brandies and all.
But California is distinguished for quality as well as for quantity. Not that a high proportion of total production can be classed with cognac or armagnac as the finest and most subtle of after-dinner liqueurs, but virtually all Californian brandy is carefully made and matured, and the light-bodied fruity style of most brands lends itself to mixing – most Americans take their brandy mixed, as the basis for cocktails and for long drinks such as brandy sours.

South-American Pisco and Californian brandy. California is one of the world's greatest brandy-producing regions, distinguished for quality.

a   b   c

The glasses for these long and short drinks are of all shapes and sizes, but it may be as well here to comment on those that should be used for the finest after-dinner brandies.

It is an affectation to serve such delicacies in balloon glasses the size of one's head, or of a goldfish bowl.

The type most favoured in good Paris restaurants and in Cognac itself, whether in the tasting-room or at table, is a moderate-sized (about 12 cm. high, or a shade more) slightly tapering glass very like a sherry *copita* (see drawing a). Other shapes to be met in Cognac, though not so frequently, are what they call a tulip (b) and a very small *ballon* (c) of roughly the same capacity as either of the others.

All these are big enough to be filled only about one-quarter full, so that there is room for the aromatic vapours to collect and be sniffed, and small enough to be

cradled in the hand for its warmth gently to release such fragrance.
Brandy glasses should never be warmed over a spirit-lamp, as in some flashily pretentious restaurants: the warmth of the hand is enough. And to burn methylated spirits in the presence of a fine brandy is, in any case, an act of folly.

Not that this is the only way to take cognac. At the turn of the century, there was an elderly uncle of Oscar Wilde who was a great devotee of the finest of brandies. One day there was a fire at his house, put out with dash and daring by a fireman for whom the old gentleman, overcome with gratitude, poured out an enormous glass of his grandest and rarest. The fireman, busy removing his wet boots and socks, thanked him kindly, observing that, 'I'm a teetotaler myself, sir, but I've always found that there's nothing like brandy for preventing a cold', and poured the lot over his feet.

The 'balloon'-shaped cognac glass has to be small enough to be cradled in the hand so that it can be warmed evenly.

4   Malt and Grain

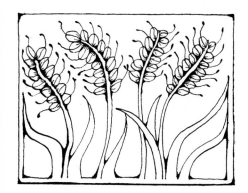

The origins of whisky are lost, if not in an alcoholic haze, at any rate in the mists of time.

It is generally supposed, though there are no grounds for anything stronger than supposition, that in the western world it was the Irish who first distilled spirits from grain as distinct from grapes and other fruit, and that the art or craft of distilling was taken from Ireland to Scotland in the early middle ages. (What we now know as Scotland was inhabited originally by Picts: the Scots took themselves, their Gaelic language, and their own name and that of whisky – uisge beatha, usquebaugh, water of life – from Ireland to North Britain in the fifth century A.D.)

But if it was the Irish who invented whisky, it was the Scots who made it world-famous, and any chapter on whisky must begin with Scotch.

Let it be noticed here that the Scots themselves approve the adjective 'Scotch' only for whisky and broth: they prefer 'Scots' and 'Scottish' in all other senses. And be it noted, too, that Scotch whisky (and Canadian) has no 'e': Irish and American whiskeys do.

In the beginning, there was malt whisky. This was how it was made – and how, in essentials, it is made to this day.

Barley is caused to germinate by steeping it in water and by heating: each grain sprouts little rootlets, like those of potatoes left too long in the larder. The starch in the grain has become sugar, which ferments into alcohol.

Germination is checked by drying over a fire – traditionally, over a fire of peat, which imparts some of its aroma and flavour to the malted barley and thus, eventually, to the whisky.

The dried malted barley is mashed into a liquor to which yeast is added, and the resultant fermented liquid is distilled in an old-fashioned pot still (see chapter 3 for the difference between pot still and patent still) to produce a spirit which in varying degrees, according to the part of Scotland it comes from, the size and shape of the still in which it was distilled, and the nature of the water, the peat and the cask in which it matured, will offer to nose and to palate some of the richness of the malt, some of the softness of the water, some of the smoky aroma of the peat fire. This is pot still whisky, of which more anon, after we have recorded the importance in the history of whisky of the invention of the patent still.

In 1826, Robert Stein (Stein is a Scottish, as well as a German surname) invented a patent still for the rapid distillation of grain spirit. In 1830 or 1833, Aeneas Coffey, formerly Inspector-General of Irish Excise, patented a better one. Now, it became possible to produce more spirit, more quickly and more cheaply, from unmalted grain – a spirit that derived no flavour from malt and none from peat, but a virtually neutral, or 'silent' spirit, such as vodka, or such as is flavoured to become gin, a spirit referred to as grain whisky to distinguish it from malt whisky.

It took half a century or so, but the introduction of the patent still and its grain whisky revolutionised the drinking habits of the English middle and upper classes and, eventually, those of the western world.

Writing in 1930 of his adventures as a young cavalry officer on the North-West Frontier of India, Winston Churchill recorded that it was in September 1898, waiting to go into action with the

The processes that go to the distilling of Scotch whisky.

BARLEY STORE	MALTING		
	Steeps 3 days	Maltings 8–12 days	Peat kiln 2 days

Malakand Field Force, that he overcame his 'repugnance to the taste of whisky', adding that 'to this day [1930] I have never shrunk when occasion warranted it from the main basic standing refreshment of the white officer in the East.'

The historic relevance of this story is that, as Winston Churchill pointed out, 'of course all this whisky business was quite a new departure in fashionable England. My father for instance could never have drunk whisky except when shooting on a moor or in some very dull chilly place. He lived in the age of the "brandy and soda".'

The change thus recorded by so good an authority on the social history of our recent past was not, as such changes can be and often are, a matter of chance or of whim. For increasingly, during the decades before those frontier skirmishes of the eighteen-nineties, Scottish distillers had been blending with their hearty, pungently aromatic, pot still malt whiskies – whiskies suitable for

Scottish landscape. The fullness of the malted barley, the softness of the water and the flavour of burned peat contribute to the unique quality of Scotch whisky.

...SHING	FERMENTA-TION	DISTILLATION			MATURA-TION	BLENDING
...ll	Mash tun 8 hours *springwater	Still 1st distillation 6 hours	Still 2nd distillation 8 hours	Receiver	Cask minimum 5 years	Bottling
	Washback 2–3 days					Packing

Whisky distilleries in Scotland

1 Highland Park
2 Scapa
3 Pulteney
4 Brora
5 Clynelish
6 Balblair
7 Glenmorangie
8 Dalmore
9 Teaninich
10 Ben Wyvis
11 Invergordon
13 Glenlassaugh
14 Macduff
15 Banff
16 Glen Moray-Glenlivet
17 Linkwood
18 Miltonduff-Glenlivet
19 Glenburgie-Glenlivet
20 Mannochmore
21 Benriach-Glenlivet
22 Longmorn-Glenlivet
23 Glenlossie
24 Benromach
25 Dallas Dhu
26 Glen Elgin
27 Coleburn
28 Royal Brackla
29 Ord
30 Knockdhu
31 Auchroisk
32 Glentauchers
33 Aultmore
34 Glen Keith-Glenlivet
35 Strathisla-Glenlivet
36 Strathmill
37 Caperdonich
38 Glen Grant-Glenlivet
39 Glenrothes-Glenlivet
40 Glen Spey
41 Speyburn
42 Craigellachie
43 Glen Albyn
44 Glen Mhor
45 Millburn
46 Cardow
47 Macallan
48 Aberlour-Glenlivet
49 Knockando
50 Tamdhu-Glenlivet
51 Imperial
52 Dailuaine
53 Glenallachie
54 Benrinnes
55 Convalmore
56 Glendullan
57 Mortlach
58 Balvenie
59 Glenfiddich
60 Dufftown-Glenlivet
61 Pittyvaich-Glenlivet
62 Glendronach
63 Glenfarclas-Glenlivet
64 Cragganmore
65 Tomintoul-Glenlivet
66 Allt a Bhainne
67 Tormore
68 Ardmore
69 Talisker
70 Tomatin
71 The Glenlivet
72 Balmenach
73 Tamnavulin-Glenlivet
74 Braes of Glenlivet
75 Glenugie
76 Glengarioch
77 Lochnagar

78 Glenury-Royal
79 Dalwhinnie
80 Ben Nevis
81 Glenlochy
82 Fettercairn
83 Brechin (North Port)
84 Glencadam
85 Hillside
86 Lochside
87 Blair Athol
88 Edradour
90 Aberdeldy
91 Oban
92 Glenturret
93 Tullibardine
94 Deanston
95 Cameronbridge
96 Cambus
97 North of Scotland
98 Carsebridge
99 Glengoyne
100 Loch Lomond
101 Bunnahabhain
102 Dumbarton
103 Inverleven
104 Lomond
105 Littlemill
106 Auchentoshan
107 Rosebank
108 St. Magdalene
109 Caledonian
110 North British
111 Glenkinchie
112 Moffat
113 Kinclaith

114 Port Dundas
115 Strathclyde
116 Caol Ila
117 Isle of Jura
118 Bruichladdich
119 Bowmore
120 Ardbeg
121 Port Ellen

122 Lagavulin
123 Laphroaig
124 Glen Scotia
125 Springbank
126 Girvan
127 Ladyburn
128 Bladnoch

Information from The Whisky Map of Scotland, published in Scotland by John Bartholomew & Sons, Edinburgh.

46

grouse-moors and for deer-stalking, but too heavy for Victorian drawing-rooms – the lighter, drier, more nearly neutral patent still grain whiskies.

At first, patent still grain whisky was looked at askance and so, too, were blends of patent still grain and pot still malt. The distillers of patent still grain combined in 1877 to form The Distillers Company and to battle against those who denied, in pamphlets and in Parliament, that grain whisky was entitled to be called whisky at all, and against the book especially sponsored by the Irish distillers, 'to check the practices of the fraudulent traders by whom silent spirit' [i.e. neutral spirit, or tasteless alcohol], 'variously disguised and flavoured, is sold under the name of Whisky'.

The thunder of battle was to reverberate into the twentieth century, but in effect the war was won and lost in 1891, when a Select Committee set up by Parliament reported that 'it is stated that public taste requires whiskey [sic] of less marked characteristics than formerly, and to gratify this desire, various blends are made, either by the mixture of pot still products, or by the addition of silent spirit from the patent stills…' The Committee decided that the addition of patent still spirit would be regarded not as an adulteration but as a dilution and therefore legal.

The new sort of Scotch whisky vastly extended its empire – almost entirely as the basis of a mixed drink, usually a long mixed drink: Scotch and water; Scotch and soda; Scotch, eventually, on the rocks.

It was partly that the lighter blend was eminently acceptable to sedentary southerners, for whom Highland malts had proved too heavy. It was partly the go-ahead marketing methods of the men who were soon to become a whole generation of racehorse-owning whisky barons. It was partly that it all happened

at a time when there was a shortage of good brandy because of the phylloxera plague in France, and too great an abundance of bad brandy to take its place. Whisky was better.

(Cognac, ousted from its role as a mixer, in 'B. and S.', made a magnificent come-back as the lordliest of after-dinner drinks, in Britain actually challenging vintage port itself, as whisky had so successfully challenged brandy for pre-prandial honours.)

Today, there has been a revival of interest in malt whisky, whether single-malt – which is to say the malt of one distillery only – or blended or vatted malt, which is to say a blend of different malts, but without any grain. They are drunk straight, as liqueurs, after dinner, or as the Scots themselves do, as aperitifs or between-meals drinks, with about the same amount of plain water – never with soda.

Nevertheless, they are a minority taste, and most of the production of malt whisky goes to the widely advertised, world famous, branded blends: White Label and White Horse, for instance; Johnny Walker and J. and B. Rare; Bell's and Teacher's and the rest.

The blends differ from each other not only according to the relative proportions of malt and grain, but to the relative proportions of the different malts. Usually, a typical blended whisky of commerce will consist of about forty per cent malt whisky to sixty per cent grain, but the difference can be as much as the other way round. There is no doubt that the tendency in recent years has been to increase the proportion of grain.

Malt whisky is the more expensive of the two: blends with more malt than grain will be found among the premium or de luxe brands, such as Chivas Regal and Johnny Walker Black Label, and be fuller in flavour. Which is not necessarily to say that some of the light, dry brands, blended to the modern taste such as J. and B. Rare, are high in grain, low in malt. It is claimed for such brands, though without supporting figures, that specially light, delicate malts are selected, so as to give flavour without heaviness. (See chapter 3: compare with Delamain 'Pale and Dry' cognac.)

Whereas there are about 3,000 brands of blended Scotch whisky on the market, there are 117 malts, traditionally classified as Highland malts (the vast majority) from north of an imaginary line drawn from Glasgow to Dundee; Lowland malts, from south of that line to the English border; and Campbeltown and Islay malts, from the Mull of Kintyre peninsula and the island of Islay respectively, off the south-west coast of Scotland. Whiskies from the Orkney islands are included in the Highland malts. Every one is different from the others, but generally speaking the Highland malts are more flavoury than the Lowland malts, the Campbeltown and Islay malts heavier than either.

49

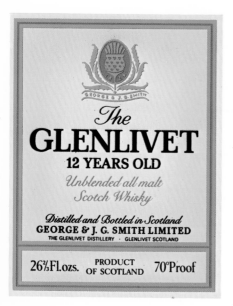

The
GLENLIVET
12 YEARS OLD
*Unblended all malt
Scotch Whisky*

Distilled and Bottled in Scotland
GEORGE & J. G. SMITH LIMITED
THE GLENLIVET DISTILLERY · GLENLIVET SCOTLAND

26⅔Fl.ozs. | PRODUCT OF SCOTLAND | 70°Proof

Some Highland malts are especially famous: The Glenlivet is entitled by law to the definite article, which distinguishes it from the thirty others with 'Glenlivet' as part of a hyphenated name. Only five per cent of its production is bottled as a single malt – the rest goes to the blenders, as does 95 per cent of Glenfiddich, the most widely advertised single Highland malt.

It is the malt whiskies that give a Scotch whisky blend its character, and the water and the peat that give character to malt whisky. The barley for malting may come from as far away as Australia, but Australia could not make a malt whisky. Or so the Scots say.

Grain whisky is made in Scotland from maize, much of it these days, if not indeed most of it, imported from Central Europe. As its character does not depend on peat and water, and as it is a more or less neutral spirit, it can be produced anywhere in the world.

All this being so, it will be easily understood why countries skilled in distilling, whether the skill is traditional, as in Holland, or newly acquired, as in Japan, can import malt whisky from Scotland and blend it with home-produced grain whisky to make a perfectly sound blend of 'Scotch' (except that they may not call it so, though nothing stands in the way of a Scottish sounding brand-name, or a tartan background to the label.)

The export of malt whisky by some Scottish distillers, particularly to Japan, Brazil and Argentina, has been denounced by others as 'suicidal' and as 'giving your enemy a razor and inviting him to cut your throat'.

Certainly, I have tasted both Dutch and Japanese whiskies, blending domestic grain with imported Scottish malts, that were admirable Scotch-type whiskies by any standard, and Japan, at any rate, is now producing some malt whisky as well

as grain. There are some pessimists in Scotland who have their doubts as to the inimitability of Scottish peat, Scottish water and Scottish skill – the three elements peculiar so far to pot still malt – and who have prophesied in the trade press that by the nineteen-eighties Japan will be producing not only its own grain and a little malt, but all the malt whisky it needs. Which makes one wonder about Scottish faith in the inimitability of Scotch malt whisky.

There was a time, up to about the eighteen-eighties, when Irish was the aristocrat of whiskies, and blended Scotch a vulgar *arriviste*. But Irish distillers were slower than the Scots to move with the times. Skilful marketing gave Scotch whisky the advantage, and by the time Prohibition hit the United States it was Scotch, and never Irish, for which bootleggers risked their freedom, their fortunes, and sometimes even their lives.
Scotch whisky achieved a place in the American way of life that it has never lost.

Today, the Irish whiskey industry has rationalised itself. There are two major distilling firms: one, in Northern Ireland, producing Old Bushmills, and one in the Republic producing John Jameson, Power's and other brands. Generally speaking, although Irish whiskey is now a blend, like Scotch, of malt and grain, it is maltier in style and notably softer,

51

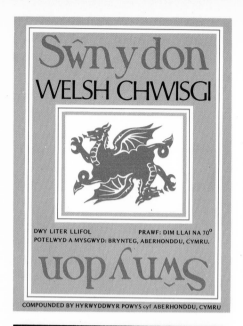

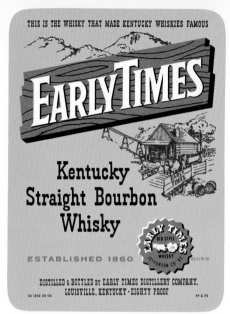

THIS IS THE WHISKY THAT MADE KENTUCKY WHISKIES FAMOUS

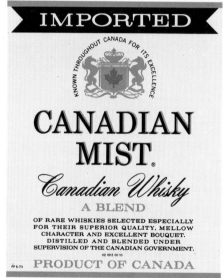

Unlike Scotch, the various north-American whiskeys are less well-known abroad than in their own countries: Americans abroad are more likely to ask for Scotch than for Bourbon or rye or Canadian Club. But the United States Government officially recognises no fewer than thirty-three distinct types of American whiskey, of which two at least are classics.

Of these two main types, Bourbon, named after Bourbon county in the state of Kentucky, is distilled from a mash of grain that must consist of at least 51 per cent corn (maize) but more usually consists of about 60 per cent – the other grain may be rye and/or barley – and matured in barrels of charred oak. One Bourbon whiskey blended with another Bourbon whiskey becomes Blended Straight Bourbon: blended with other, usually neutral, spirit it becomes the lighter Blended Bourbon. Most Bourbon is made by the 'sweet mash' process: yeast is added to set off fermentation.

In the 'sour mash' process, fermentation is induced by the residue of a previous fermentation. This produces a finer whiskey that is fuller in flavour and fragrance – and more expensive. Just as Bourbon or Blended Straight Bourbon is heavier than Blended Bourbon, rye is heavier still – made from a mash containing at least 51 per cent rye, and not unlike Irish whiskey in flavour and aroma. The same rule as to blends applies as for Bourbon.

a notable amateur of whisky has told me, compared with the lighter, sharper, Scotch. Some old Irish whiskeys still obtainable may date from the time, twenty years or so ago, when there were blends of malt whiskeys only – no grain – and are after-dinner liqueurs of remarkable individuality and charm.

And it must not go unrecorded here that the other part of Britain's Celtic fringe, Wales, which once tried to make a whisky

of its own and failed, has now decided to try again. Chwisgi Cymraeg, or Welsh whisky, is now on sale in Welsh pubs under the brand name of Swn y Don, Sound of the Waves, and is said to resemble a lightish Scotch whisky, such as might be compounded of light Lowland malt and grain. With a production at present of 1200 bottles a month, Wales seems hardly likely to bring the Scotch whisky industry to its knees…

Of the whiskies of the world, undeniably Scotch dominates the field: historically and traditionally, Irish is usually given second place, though not quantitively. But in the USA, American whiskey, in its many styles, is the most important spirit, and Bourbon is a global export. Canadian whisky is also world-renowned. The newcomer, Japanese whisky, should no longer be ignored.

Rye was born in Pennsylvania and did perhaps as much as the Winchester and the Colt to open up the West. Bourbon belongs more to the South and is the classic base for the equally classic long, refreshing mint julep, for which Virginia claims the credit – Kentucky being content with having created Bourbon itself.

Indeed, there is a story of a Virginian who persuaded a Kentucky friend to make a julep of his Bourbon; some months later, the Kentuckian's butler was found grieving at his master's graveside, explaining 'A gemmun from Virginny done showed Massa how to eat grass in his whiskey, and Massa done ate himself to death!'

Canadian whisky is more like rye than Bourbon, more like Irish than Scotch, but lighter than any of them. Its making and marketing are as strictly controlled by the Canadian government as is the production of cognac by the French.

Other grain Spirits: Gin, Vodka, Aquavit and others

Half a century or so ago, an aged ex-professor of Rhetoric and English Literature in the University of Edinburgh, George Saintsbury, wrote of gin as 'the most specifically English of all spirits', but the truth is that the story of gin begins not in England but, certainly, in the Netherlands, possibly in the sixteenth century, and probably at Leyden, not yet itself, but soon to become, a university town.

It was there, it is said, that an apothecary, having first experimented with steeping juniper berries in wine, as the French were already doing, turned to re-distilling a neutral spirit with the berries, for medicinal purposes – certainly as a diuretic, and probably, in those credulous days, as a magic cure-all.

It seems soon to have become much more even than that, if the legend is true that the thousand horsemen and five thousand foot whom Queen Elizabeth despatched to the Low Countries in 1585 to fight against Philip of Spain came back marvelling at the 'Dutch courage' shown by their comrades-in-arms, and bearing it with them in bottles...

Soon, the envious English were distilling it for themselves. Stuart monarchs gave leave to brewers to distil spirits from English grain, and a Worshipful Company of Distillers was added to the list of London's ancient livery companies. It was not, however, until 1688, a century later, with the accession of Dutch William to the English throne, that gin became fully established in England.

As a result of William's wars against Louis XIV of France, it was forbidden to import French brandy, and gin became the patriotic spirit to drink, in the same way that port, from England's ally, Portugal, became the patriotic alternative to French claret.

It was about this time, in the early eighteenth century, that what the author of *Robinson Crusoe* had referred to as 'the new-fashioned compound waters called Geneva' came to be known in England as gin – a derivation from the Dutch *genever,* as that in turn derived from the Old French *genevre* (modern French, *genièvre*) from the Latin *juniperus.*

To this day, the informing flavour of the juniper berry gives both the English and the Dutch gins not only their tastes but their names, though the two spirits differ from each other both in style and in the ways they are taken.

Dutch gin (sometimes known abroad as 'Hollands', more rarely as 'Schiedam', and always on its native heath as 'genever') is based on a spirit distilled, like malt whisky and cognac, in old-fashioned pot stills and, again like malt whisky, from malted grain, wholly or partly. This gives it from the beginning a greater intensity of flavour than English gin, which begins as a much more nearly neutral spirit – like grain whisky, not malt – made in a continuous patent still, and from any unmalted grain, or any other vegetable matter rich in starch. (Alcohol can be distilled from any vegetable matter containing sugar, or starch, which converts into sugar. During the war, when wheat was scarce in Britain – imported at the cost of sailors' lives – English gin was made from English potatoes. But this is a costly and cumbersome method in peacetime. (A potable spirit can be made from sawdust, but this is more cumbersome and costly still.) Dutch gin's intensity of flavour is made greater still by the fact that the spirit is re-distilled with its 'botanicals' – juniper

quarrel with those of any such mixers, as vermouth or quinine tonic-water. In Germany (where any strong, dry spirit is known generically as schnapps, whether it is aquavit or gin, kirschwasser or vodka) spirits are distilled that are closely akin to Dutch gins.

Steinhaeger, produced in Westphalia, has a particularly strong flavour of juniper, for it is distilled from the fermented berries themselves – not made by flavouring a more or less neutral spirit. It has consequently proved a disappointment in many a British or American army officers' mess in Germany where they have thought to use it as the British and the Americans do their own gin at home – with tonic water or in a Martini. In its own right, taken neat, like Dutch gin, it is as honest and hearty as the sturdy stoneware flagon in which it is usually sold.

The malting of the grain, where the production of genever starts.

The juniper berry, which gave its name to Dutch genever and English gin.

berries or their oil, coriander, the peels of various citrus fruits, cassia, orris root, barks, seeds and other flavourings, in proportions that depend on the house-style of the particular distillery. English gins use similar 'botanicals' but infused rather than re-distilled, and again in differing proportions.

Dutch genever, therefore, is highly aromatic to the nose, full in the mouth – to be drunk neat and not as a basis for mixed drinks, for its taste and smell would

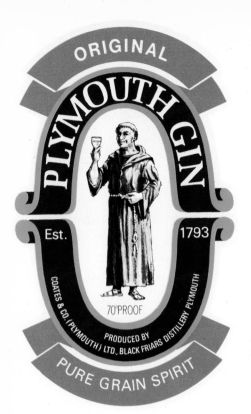

English gin (and the same type is distilled in many other countries, especially in the United States and even in Holland), is much lighter, both in flavour and in fragrance, and is rarely drunk neat but either with bitters or, more usually, as a basis for cocktails, especially with vermouth, and as a long drink with flavoured bottled waters or fruit squashes or juice.

So far, we have referred to 'English' gin as distinct from Dutch, but this type is universally marketed and known as London dry gin. (It is, in fact, sweetened but relatively slightly.) 'London' defines style, not provenance.
A sweeter version, made in England but now better-known abroad, is Old Tom. The original gin sling (a long drink involving lime-juice, various sweet liqueurs, ice, soda-water, orange and mint, as well as gin) used to be known as a 'Tom Collins' because it was made with Old Tom, unlike a 'John Collins', which was not. Now, though, the

distinction is forgotten; London gin is often used for either; and the names have become more or less interchangeable. In England, the usual way to take a gin sling is in the form of a Pimm's No. 1 – a bottled concentrate to which fizzy lemonade is added. Indeed, the words 'gin sling' are forgotten, and it is Pimm's No. 1 that is called for, as such. When champagne is used instead of lemonade, the drink becomes a Pimm's Royal. I advise sweet champagne for this. Plymouth gin is not sweetened any more than London gin is, but is heavier and more pungent – half-way to Dutch. Not so heavily flavoured, though, that it cannot be used as a mixer: there are those, indeed – sailors, especially and, naturally enough, the distillers of Plymouth gin – who insist that pink gin, which consists of gin, water, ice and a dash of Angostura bitters, and is the traditional aperitif of British naval officers, should always be made with Plymouth gin, never with London.

Students of the subject who are not so partisan hold that either will do: made with the pungent Plymouth, a pink gin tastes more of gin – made with the lighter London, more of bitters.

When the Dutch themselves look to gin as a basis for a cocktail or a long mixed drink, they call for a dry gin in the London style – though it may well be from a Dutch distillery. Otherwise, they drink, neat and ice-cold, with their raw or pickled or marinaded herring hors d'oeuvre, either 'jong' (young) Dutch gin or, less and less frequently these days, the 'old' genever which is not necessarily longer-matured, but made to seem so in character – straw-coloured, a shade sweeter, a shade less strong in alcohol, and even more aromatic than the young gin. The Dutch distilleries, among which are some of the biggest and oldest in the world, also produce various flavoured gins, drier enough in style than the richly sweet fruit cordials discussed in later chapters for many Dutch folk to drink them as aperitifs, but appealing to some sophisticated tastes as sweet and fruity enough to drink after dinner, while being far less cloying than the usual fruit liqueurs.

They are based, of course, on a dry gin of the London type, not on the traditional genever. Indeed, one old-fashioned Dutch distiller even says of them that they are fruit vodkas rather than fruit gins, because the basic spirit is so much more

flown with claret and flushed with port: miners and millhands and their wives tumbled into the gutters sodden with gin.

It was of the London of the eighteen-thirties that Charles Dickens wrote in his *Sketches by Boz* that gin-palaces 'are invariably numerous and splendid in proportion to the dirt and poverty of the surrounding neighbourhood. The gin-shops in and near Drury Lane, Holborn, St. Giles's,

Most of the Dutch distilleries pride themselves on a history dating from the seventeenth century, the Dutch Golden Age.

nearly neutral than what he regards as true gin.

However that may be, all Holland knows them as gins – to quote the most widely marketed of them, as citroengenever (lemon) and bessengenever (black currant) and very good they are, whether regarded as gins or as vodkas.

When old George Saintsbury, ignoring both Holland and Hollands, wrote of gin as being so 'specifically English' he felt also obliged to say that it was a 'humble and much reviled liquid'.

For, unlike Dutch gin in its native country, London gin throughout the eighteenth and nineteenth centuries had been the means by which the earliest exploited victims of the Industrial Revolution had anaesthetised themselves – their only way of escape from drudgery and squalor.

The country gentlemen and the new squirearchy of ironmasters and coalowners fell under their mahogany

VOGUE

Early August Issue 1926

ONE SHILLING

Condé Nast & Co Ltd Proprietors

The Cocktail Age of the nineteen-twenties suddenly made gin leap into respectability. Of all the cocktails of that time in fact only the Dry Martini and long drinks such as gin fizzes have survived. Cover of Vogue from 1926.

Covent Garden and Clare Market are the handsomest in London. There is more of filth and squalid misery near those great thoroughfares than in any part of this mighty city'.

But Saintsbury, in the nineteen-twenties, was writing on the eve of London gin's sudden leap into respectability. We talk now of the middle nineteen-twenties as 'the Cocktail Age'.
Not that either the name or the nostrum was unknown before then: the preface to Jerry Thomas's classic *How to Mix Drinks, or the Bon-Vivant's Companion*, published in New York in 1862, no doubt to bolster Yankee morale after Bull Run, records 'a small drinking saloon' having been set up in London, near the Bank of England, 'by a peripatetic American' and observes that 'the "Connecticut eyeopener" and "Alabama fog-cutters", together with the "lightning smashes" and "thunderbolt cocktails" created a profound sensation…'

No recipe is given for any of these nectars, and we do not know, therefore, whether any of them was based on gin. What is certain is that 'cocktails' did not catch on, and that it was not until 1924 or 1925, according to Alec Waugh, the novelist and a knowledgeable and perceptive historian of the times, that the first 'cocktail parties', thus styled, were held in London.
The first 'cocktails' were, in fact, Alec Waugh recalls, rum swizzles, but soon virtually all the mixed-up drinks for the mixed-up drinkers of the Cocktail Age were based on gin.
True, one or two have survived that are based on brandy and Cointreau, such as the White Lady and the Sidecar, but the Monkey Gland and Mah Jongg, Between the Sheets and Bosom Caresser – even, heaven preserve us, the League of Nations – all or most of them based on gin, have gone the way of those named after the stars of the silent films of the time: Mary Pickford and Douglas Fairbanks, Will Rogers and the Gish Sisters.

61

Gammal Norrlands Akvav
Herrgårds Aquav
OP Anderson Aquav
Reimersholms Aquav
Overste Brännvi
Skåne Akvav
Punsc

Gammel Løitens Aquavit • Oslo
Lysholm Linie Aquavit

• Aalborg

Aalborgs Jubilaeums Akvavit
Aalborg Akvavit

Copenhagen •

Bommerlunder

• Flensburg

Kornbrand
Edelkorn
Eiskorn

Weser

Elbe

Oder

Berlin •

London Gin
• London

Jonge jenever
Oude jenever
Bessenjenever
Citroenjenever

• Amsterdam

• Schiedam

Steinhäger
Schinkenhäger

• Steinhagen

Thames

Plymouth Gin
• Plymouth

Jenever
• Hasselt •
Brussels

Bonn •

Meuse

Rhein

Main

Prague •

Seine

Paris
•

Loire

Donau

62

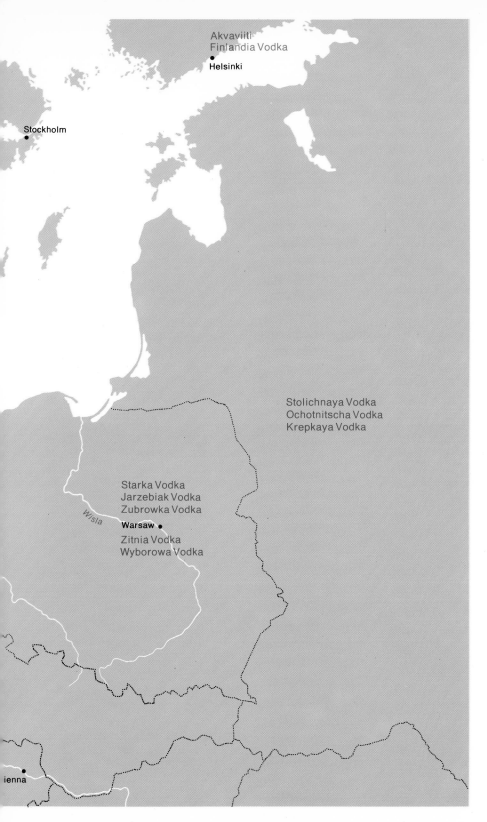

Akvaviiti
Finlandia Vodka
● Helsinki

● Stockholm

Stolichnaya Vodka
Ochotnitscha Vodka
Krepkaya Vodka

Starka Vodka
Jarzebiak Vodka
Zubrowka Vodka

Wisla

Warsaw ●

Zitnia Vodka
Wyborowa Vodka

ienna ●

As we shall see later, there are widely-known mixed drinks these days based on rum and on vodka, but of the gin-based descendants of those Connecticut eye-openers of a century ago, and the Bosom Caressers of those between-the-wars days of cloche hats and the Charleston, few are left save the Martini or, more particularly, the Dry Martini.

Time was when a Martini was simply half-and-half London gin and French (which is to say dry, white) vermouth, and a Dry Martini two of gin to one of French. (Whoever calls nowadays for that favourite of fifty years ago, a gin-and-It?) I recall, though, an article in an American magazine entitled *172 Ways to Make a Martini,* one recipe counselling 'keeping the vermouth in a separate room and bringing it within three feet of the gin at cocktail hour', which makes Ernest Hemingway's fifteen of gin to one of vermouth look like an infant's posset... But a whole learned (and very lively) book has been written about this one drink and I need do no more than refer the serious student to John Doxat's *Stirred – Not Shaken.*

Thanks to the Martini and to such long drinks as gin-and-tonic and gin-and-lime, London gin still holds a major place in world markets and in the world's bars, in spite of the passing of the cocktail craze and in spite, too, of the Western world's more recent love affair with vodka.

Not all that long ago, vodka was a legend in the West: there was a brief period of euphoric fraternisation at the end of the war in Europe when British, French and American officers, inured to and immune from the effects of whisky-and-sodas, Pernods and ten-to-one Martinis, would fall stupefied under the table when plied with vodka by their Soviet comrades-in-arms.

It was the legend rather than the liquor that did the trick, and the legend is far older than the Second World War – far, far older than the Iron Curtain.

Under the Czars or under the Commissars, Russia in the eyes of the West has always been a mysterious place: 'a riddle wrapped in a mystery inside an enigma', in Winston Churchill's words, and vodka was for long credited with a mysterious potency.

There were those, even, who seriously maintained that the Russian Revolution was brought about by a Czarist banning of vodka as a wartime measure, and that it became as bloody as it did because the Reds made up for lost drinking-time. Nonsense, of course, though it is true that some things are too sacred for even an all-powerful state to interfere with, as Lenin himself discovered. Attempting to continue, after the 1917 revolution, the imperial ban of 1914, he found workers and peasants sulkily recalcitrant and submitted to the will of the people with a resigned, 'Drunkenness is better than slavery!'

But vodka has always loomed large in Russian history: Peter the Great, writing to his wife from Paris in 1716, complained, 'There is only one bottle of vodka left: I don't know what to do...' And just as Peter had made the uncouth Russian courtiers shave their beards, so his niece, the Empress Anne, taught the ladies of the imperial court to wash their hair in a solution of logwood in vodka – and then drink it.

Disentangle it from the myths and legends that attach themselves to it, and vodka is not really mysterious at all. Its name means nothing more than 'little water', and it is a simple and straightforward spirit that has been distilled in Russia, Poland and Finland since time immemorial, from any form of fermentable carbohydrate – preferably grain and, among the grains, usually from wheat, corn or rye. (Vodka can be, and sometimes is, distilled from potatoes, as gin was in England during the war, when grain was hard to come by, and as aquavit is in Scandinavia, where potatoes are

Vodka, the drink of Czars, peasants and workers, has always loomed large in Russian history. A vodka bottle from 1886 and vodka carafes and glasses from 1836.

Vodka bottles from Czarist times.

more plentiful than grain, but you get less vodka per pound of potatoes than per pound of grain.)

The Russian way with what has come to be regarded as the Russian national drink is to take it well-chilled, tossed off neat at a gulp from a very small glass, or silver jigger, and with salty, fishy, greasy *zakouski*, which are hors-d'oeuvre, such as caviar and salt herring.

I refer to it as Russian, not as Soviet, for vodka came originally from Russia proper (chiefly, indeed, from around Leningrad, where the water of the lakes is said to be the softest in all the Russias, ideal both for distillation and for dilution to drinkable strength). Thus, it is unlike the wines of the Union, which come from the southern constituent republics, chiefly Georgia, Armenia and the Ukraine, and which it is as wrong to call 'Russian' as it would be to speak of 'English whisky' – they are Soviet, but not Russian, just as Scotch whisky and Irish whiskey are British but not English. Now the use of vodka has spread all over the Union, just as whisky has spread all over the United Kingdom, and yet, common as it is, there is still a ceremonial about the way in which it is served. In the better restaurants there are heavily cut little glasses for it, the size of liqueur glasses, sometimes with clear cutting through coloured glass, like the old fashioned hock glasses, or Baccarat overlay paperweights. And every fancy shop in Moscow and Leningrad sells pretty little vodka cups in coloured enamel on silvergilt, or in silver deeply engraved, like the back of a Victorian watch.

In spite of the legend, vodka need be no stronger than gin or whisky, and outside its native countries it rarely is: of the British-made brands, the more popular of the two Smirnoff varieties is 65 degrees, and Relska 65.5 – standard gins and whiskies are 70 degrees, the same as the standard Stolichnaya vodka imported from the Soviet Union. Though there are stronger vodkas to be had, of course, most of them Polish. Indeed, there is a Polish top-of-the-head remover, recommended only to serious students, called Pure Polish Spirit, 140 degrees proof – absolute alcohol being 175.1 – of which it was once observed that it was the cheapest and handiest method, since the virtual disappearance of the French Foreign Legion of legend, of not remembering whatever it was that men used to go to Sidi-bel-Abbes to forget. And there is a Polish Vodka Starka, which is made from rye and not, like most Russian vodka, from wheat, aged in cask to a pale straw colour and a slight tang of sherry, that reaches a formidable 87 degrees. What the Poles are particularly good at, though, is producing flavoured vodkas on a commercial scale, whereas the Russians drink theirs unflavoured, or flavour their own at home by steeping herbs or fruit or lemon-peel and the like in the local

66

flavourless vodka. Easily obtainable abroad, and at the normal 70 degrees, are Vodka Jarzebiak, slightly tinted, and flavoured by rowan berries, and the best-known of all Polish vodkas, Vodka Zubrowka, the palest possible green in shade from the zubrowka grass that gives it its fresh, clean herby taste. Finnish vodka is highly regarded by connoisseurs. Its high quality is attributed to the purity of the water used in its distillation, drawn from wells deep under the ice moraines. Such vodkas make strong, but not too strong, eye openers to toss back, ice-cold, before a meal, or with hors d'oeuvre, just as the Russians drink their own unflavoured vodkas with caviar. There is much to be said, and especially on a cold evening, for serving well-chilled vodka neat, in tiny glasses, with smoked salmon or potted shrimps.

As a rule, though, the Western way with vodka, unlike the Russian, is to use it as a mixer: not only has vodka no marked

taste of its own to quarrel with that of vermouth in a Martini, or with that of orange juice in a screwdriver, or of tomato in a Bloody Mary, or of lime or lemon and tonic water in a vodka-and-tonic, but the unflavoured alcohol vaporises and carries the scents (and, therefore, the flavours) of its mixers more easily into the nasal passages than do other, less rectified spirits.

Nor is this its only virtue. In both Britain and the United States (notably in the American *Journal of Proctology* and *The Journal of the National Medical Association*) medical men of the highest rank have produced proof that it is the congeners – fusel oil, acid, esters, aldehydes, furfural and tannins – and not the straight alcohol contained in various hard liquors that cause hangovers, and that, as a London surgeon has put it, 'the after effects of vodka (and of London gin) are substantially less than the equivalent amount of any other kind of alcoholic drink'.

And not only does vodka not affect the smell of other drinks: it does not affect the smell of the drinker, either. 'It leaves you breathless', was the slogan for one brand of vodka in the United States, but the Americans had already decided for themselves that the prime virtue of vodka was that you could get stinking and not stink.

Considering how ancient are the origins of vodka, it was long before the drink itself came west, and that it did so is largely due to the family that gives its name to the vodka most widely sold both in the United States and Britain – Smirnoff.

Vladimir Smirnoff, who, like his father and grandfather before him, had supplied vodka to t 1e imperial court, fled from the revolution of 1917 taking with him not only his wife but his almost equally precious possession, the formula for the distillation and filtration of vodka, which

FILTERED THROUGH A "MOUNTAIN" OF CHARCOAL Every drop of Smirnoff is filtered and refined through 7 tons of activated charcoal (14,000 pounds). This "black magic" removes most of the congeners so Smirnoff emerges crystal clear and flawless with no noticeable liquor taste or odor. That's why it blends so completely in fruit juices or soft drinks. Why it's dryer in Martinis and smoother on-the-rocks. Why it leaves you breathless. What's the best way to enjoy Smirnoff? *Any way that you like liquor!*

always ask for *Smirnoff* ® VODKA

I T   L E A V E S   Y O U   B R E A T H L E S S

he began to produce on a modest scale in the Paris of the nineteen-twenties. This benign figure died just before World War II, but meanwhile a fellow refugee, Rudoph Kunett, whose father had sold grain to the Smirnoff distillery, had bought the American rights. The great breakthrough in the United States came just after the war. In 1946 Jack Morgan of the Cock 'n' Bull Restaurant on Hollywood's Sunset Boulevard, anxious to sell a slow moving stock of ginger beer, cooperated with Smirnoff in an advertising campaign to promote the Moscow Mule, a potation of vodka and ginger beer. Since then, in spite of the Cold War, the traditional drink of Russia has steadily gained popularity throughout the States. Indeed, there were those in Britain who, before they succumbed themselves, used to maintain that Americans took to drinking vodka in the same way that prehistoric warriors drank the blood of their enemies. Anyway, the fashion spread from the West Coast back to Europe by way of the outlying island of Britain, soon to reach the mainland, where Pablo Picasso is said to have proclaimed that the greatest discoveries of the post-war Western World were Brigitte Bardot, modern jazz, and vodka.

A secret formula is a secret formula, but it is known that Smirnoff is made from maize and purified by filtration through charcoal, and it is supposed that the other vodkas distilled in the United States, such as Wolfschmidt, Hiram Walker, Samovar and the rest, are made in much the same way. Here, too, vodka's modern manufacture reaches back to the Saint Petersburg of the czars; for it was a chemist of that city who in 1810, a couple of years before Napoleon marched into Russia, discovered that charcoal refined, purified and softened the fiery vodka of the time more effectively than any other filtering agent. The leading Russian vodkas such as Stolichnaya – the one best known abroad – are still filtered through quartz sand and a special charcoal made from the birch trees that are so graceful a feature of the Russian landscape.

There is an old Russian phrase for vodka – 'the little ray of sunshine in the stomach' – and I have no doubt that the various Scandinavian peoples think much the same of their aquavits.

Just as the ancients named their ardent spirits *aquae vitae*, 'water of life' (though there are Italian dissidents who claim that it was really *aque di vite*, 'waters of the vine') and, as we have seen, the Irish found a name in their own outlandish language for what has become 'whisky' or 'whiskey' in ours, so the Scandinavian peoples drink each other's health in aquavit, variously spelt, according to language.

(There are some, too, and especially in Denmark, who refer to the same drink as 'snaps' or 'schnapps'.)

Originally, in the fifteenth and sixteenth centuries, aquavit was a sort of brandy, distilled from imported wine, but the Swedes took to distilling from starch-rich raw materials – first of all from grain, now to a great extent from potatoes.

Thus, it would be much like vodka were it not that it is always flavoured, and almost always with caraway. But it is drunk as vodka is drunk – ice-cold, neat, and tossed down, rather than sipped: at dinner-parties with a certain amount of ceremonial about the toastings across the table.

Like the languages of the three countries, the aquavits of Sweden, Denmark and Norway bear each a close resemblance to the other, but there are slight differences between the three and, in any one country, between various brands. Some of the Swedish aquavits are flavoured not only with caraway but also with aniseed and fennel; some of the Danish (though not Aalborg Taffel Akvavit, which is the one best-known abroad) are flavoured with cinnamon and

Akvavit: ice-cold, neat and tossed in one gulp.
A blond Scandinavian beer is a good companion.

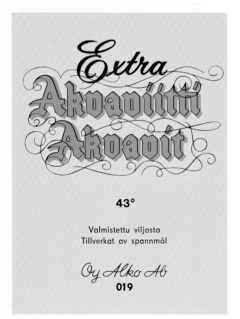

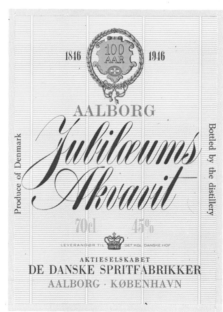

other spices. The name of one notable Norwegian brand, Linie Aquavit, indicates that it has 'crossed the Line', which is to say the Equator: it goes to Australia in oaken casks in the Wilhelmsen cargo ships and comes back a very pale golden colour and with the suggestion of sherry in its delicately subtle flavour. It is thought that the movement of the ship whilst the liquid matures in wood, or the considerable changes in temperature, or a combination of both these factors, gives an especial mellowness.

In Iceland, Sweden and Norway alcoholic liquor is a government monopoly, so there is especial authority in the advice on how to serve and drink aquavit given in a pamphlet published by the Norwegian Ministry of Foreign Affairs, no less: 'the bottle must be cold enough to be frosty with dew, the glass should be small enough to make it impossible for the dram to get lukewarm before it is finished. The newcomer who has never tasted the liquor before should not be carried away by his enthusiasm – it is a very potent drink. When it is taken with a strong, salt herring, when it is icy cold and drunk with a hearty "Skål!" – one realises why it has become the national beverage of the Norseman.'

There are debatable lands in the world of spirits and liqueurs where the cartographer is hard put to it to know where to draw his boundary lines. Saké, for instance, is a name given to both a wine made from fermented rice which, as a wine, does not concern us here, and also to a spirit distilled from rice, which does. To make confusion worse confounded, the Japanese, who ferment the one and distil the other, drink the wine as though it were tea – warm, and from porcelain cups.
I mention it among the spirits that derive from grain because of the rice, which also gives warrant for the inclusion in this chapter of arrack, a spirit that in South-east Asia may be made from the

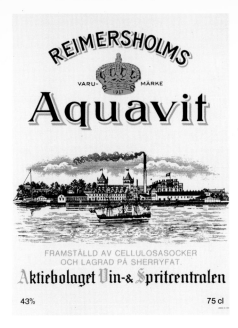

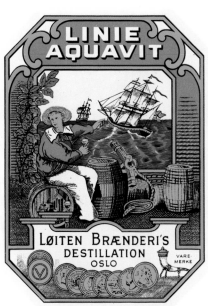

sap of the coconut palm, or from rice and sugar-cane, or from a native blossom. In the Near East the same or a similar name (such as raki) is given to spirits distilled from grain, from dates, from wine and from who knows what else : most of them, in Alexis Lichine's words, coarse drinks for rough palates. And in Java the famous Batavia Arrak has been described, not altogether helpfully, as 'a brandy-like rum'. Its chief claim to Western attention is that it forms the base for Swedish Punch, a spicy heart-warming cordial, whether taken neat after dinner as a liqueur or with hot water as a toddy.

Right : Saké, the Japanese spirit distilled from rice, is drunk as though it were tea – warm and from porcelain cups.

Because of its resemblance to the rakis of its Levantine neighbours, it is convenient to include in this chapter the ouzo of Greece, though its spirit base is as likely to be distilled from wine as from grain : it does not really matter which, for the spirit is nearly neutral, and its flavour and character derive from the seeds of the anise plant, which give it a strong smell and taste of aniseed, and the fact that its light green colour becomes opalescent as ice and water are added.

In these ways and every other it is closely related to the French (more especially southern French) descendant of the now generally forbidden absinthe – pastis, usually asked for and sold in cafés under one or other of the best-known brand-names: Pernod or Ricard.

Absinthe was devised in the eighteenth century by a not particularly ordinary Frenchman (or French Swiss) named Ordinaire, who sold the recipe to a Monsieur Pernod in 1797. It was named after one of its informing herbs – wormwood, the botanical name for which is *artemisia absinthium* – though anise was already a major consituent. Indeed, when the French government banned its production and use on 4 August 1914, the day after Germany declared war on France, and the Paris correspondent of an English newspaper was told by a horrified café-companion that 'the Star called Wormwood has fallen!' the reference was to the star-shaped seed-pods of the anise plant. The French government's ban was imposed because wormwood was considered to make men mad or vicious or both (one would have thought this favourable rather than otherwise to the French war effort) and has never been lifted. Indeed, absinthe is outlawed pretty well everywhere save in Spain, where the French firm of Pernod has a distillery that produces what one must suppose to be the old original.

Pastis is not only lacking in the wicked wormwood but is only about half so strong in alcohol as the absinthe of the good-or-bad-old-days. It is sweeter, too, and so need not have the necessary water added, drop by drop, through lumps of sugar on a perforated spoon, as used to be the ceremonial practice.

All the same, it is one of the most evocative of café-table aperitifs, as is its Greek cousin, ouzo, the smell and the taste of the one summoning up visions of the cobbled street of some Attic or Aegean-island hamlet, bleached under the blazing sky; the smell and the taste of the other recalling the click-clack-click of high heels on the Avenue des Champs-Elysées, the sight and the scent of the girls in their summer frocks, and the wish that one were a fortnight younger than one really is.

The smell and taste of Pernod, that typical French aperitif, evoke sunny terraces on the Champs-Elysées or the glory of the 'Fin de Siècle'.

6 Rum

Fifteen men on the dead man's chest –
Yo-ho-ho, and a bottle of rum!
Drink and the devil had done for the rest –
Yo-ho-ho, and a bottle of rum!

The Dead Man's Chest of the pirate song in R. L. Stevenson's *Treasure Island* is one of the tiniest of the Virgin Islands (shaped like a coffin, it is said), in the Caribbean, which is where Captain Kidd's treasure is said to be buried, and it is in the islands and on the mainland shores of the Caribbean Sea that most of the world's rum is distilled. (Batavia arrack, from Java in the East Indies, has already been referred to in chapter 5, because of its rice content.)

It has been so since the days when the Caribbean was the Spanish Main and the haunt of the pirates and buccaneers of whom E. H. Visiak, a forgotten modern English poet, wrote:

Buccaneers drinking the Devil's brew,
Here's to the King, Rum!
Here's to the Queen, Gold!
Serve we Rum
Till mouths grow mum!
Serve we gold
Till hearts grow cold!
Rum and gold 'tis sweet to follow
Till bones be bare and skulls be hollow!

A historian of piracy has recorded that in the short-lived pirate republic of Nassau, in the Bahamas, in the early eighteenth century, a favourite drink was rum and gunpowder, and a condemned pirate would honour the tradition of his trade by calling for a tumbler of rum as he stood on the gallows on Execution Dock. The origin of the name is obscure, but is said in the Oxford English Dictionary to be possibly an abbreviation of Rumbullion or Rumbustion, a surmise that does not take us very far, for the derivation of these two words is no clearer.
(Some French authorities derive 'rum' from a Malay word 'brum', which means any fermented drink. The French themselves first called the spirit of sugar-cane *guildive*, but soon took to the English word, spelling it *rhum*.)

The words were known in the mid-seventeenth century, for an account of the island of Barbados written in 1651 has it that 'the chief fudling they make in the islands is Rumbullion, alias Kill-Devill, and this is made of suggar-canes distilled, a hott, hellish and terrible liquor'.
This must have been because of crude methods of distillation and inadequate maturing, for rum as we now know it is one of the most wholesome of spirits – the spirit of sugar-cane, distilled from molasses, which is the uncrystallisable matter remaining after sugar has been produced, or directly from the sugar-cane juice before sugar production, or from a syrup of such concentrated juice.
It can be produced, like malt whisky, from the old-fashioned pot still or, like

A sugar plantation in Jamaica in the eighteenth century.

grain whisky, from the continuous patent still – as with whiskies, the heavier and more fragrant and flavourful rums from the older type of still, the lighter rums from the more modern.

Rum is a spirit uniquely close to its natural origin : it comes directly from sugar, so that there is no necessity for such a process as malting, as with malt whisky, for instance, to produce sugar from starch ; it does not have to be distilled to near-neutrality for subsequent flavouring,

as gin and vodka and aquavit; nor does it need the tannin from oak casks that gives cognac and armagnac their individuality.

Colour, though, comes from the necessary ageing, as well as from the addition of caramel, and can be intensified, as can the flavour, by adding, or redistilling with, 'congenerics', (the secondary, flavoury, constituents of the sugar-cane, largely distilled out in the basic process) or by redistilling with

'dunder', which is the solid matter left in the still after distilling – not unlike the marc left after grapes have been pressed for wine (see chapter 3).

No doubt it is the sugar content of rum (or the congenerics deriving from sugar) that gives it its warming and heartening quality. It was given to British troops in the First World War before they went 'over the top', and for nearly three hundred years the Royal Navy 'spliced the mainbrace' in rum.

At first, in the seventeenth century, British sailors were issued with a daily ration of a gallon of beer in home waters, a quart of wine in the Mediterranean, and on the West Indies station no less than half a pint of rum before noon.

It was 'new' – immature – spirit and the seamen drank it neat: his captains and ships' surgeons advised Admiral Vernon, the victor of Porto Bello, that 'it impaired their health, ruined their morals and made them slaves to every brutish passion'.

Admiral Vernon's order of 21 August 1740 that rum was no longer to be served neat but mixed with four times as much water and served in two half-issues a day has been described in the Dictionary of National Biography as 'perhaps the greatest improvement to discipline and efficiency ever produced by one stroke of the pen'.

It also gave a word to more than one language. The sailors at first resented being fobbed off with diluted drink and christened it, disparagingly, 'grog' after the admiral's boat-cloak of grogram, a rough mixture, and the admiral's nickname – 'Old Grog'. But the Admiralty approved; the grog issue spread throughout the service and became a popular and hallowed Royal Navy tradition until it was abolished in 1970 – not as an economy but because sailors in air-conditioned quarters no longer needed personal central-heating and, according to the Admiralty, because it

Even after Admiral Vernon ordered the daily ration of rum to be diluted, the Jack Tars of Nelson's time knew how to make merry on mere grog.

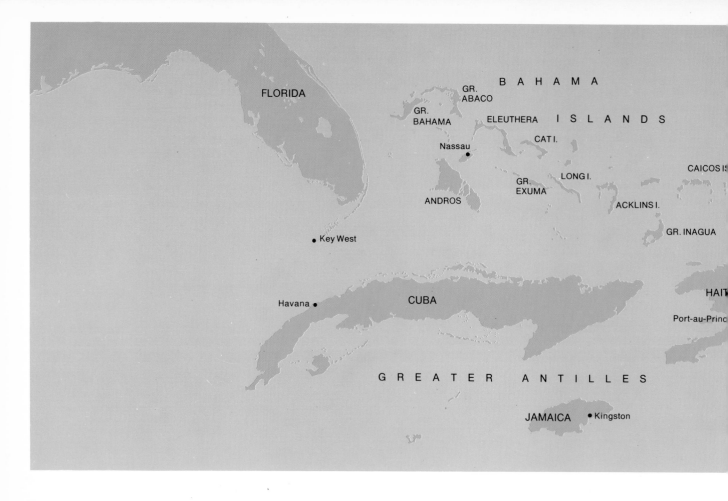

FLORIDA

B A H A M A

GR. ABACO

GR. BAHAMA

ELEUTHERA   I S L A N D S

CAT I.

Nassau

CAICOS IS

LONG I.

GR. EXUMA

ANDROS

ACKLINS I.

GR. INAGUA

Key West

CUBA

HAIT

Havana

Port-au-Princ

G R E A T E R   A N T I L L E S

JAMAICA   Kingston

was 'no longer compatible with the high standards of efficiency required in ships with complex and often delicate machinery'.

Not only is rum heart-warming in the way that seamen and soldiers have known, but the dark rums are the bases

for warm and warming cold-weather comforters, and yet have long been familiar, too, in tropical and semi-tropical climates, as long coolers.

Now, there is a vogue for particularly light rums – light in colour and in flavour – as there is for light whiskies, and these

are used not only in long, mixed cooling drinks but also in short cocktails. Traditionally, the heavier rums – thicker, sweeter, darker and more aromatic – are those of Demerara (from the banks of the river of that name in Guyana) and Jamaica, though even these two regions

The production and refinery of cane-sugar. French pictures from the eighteenth century.

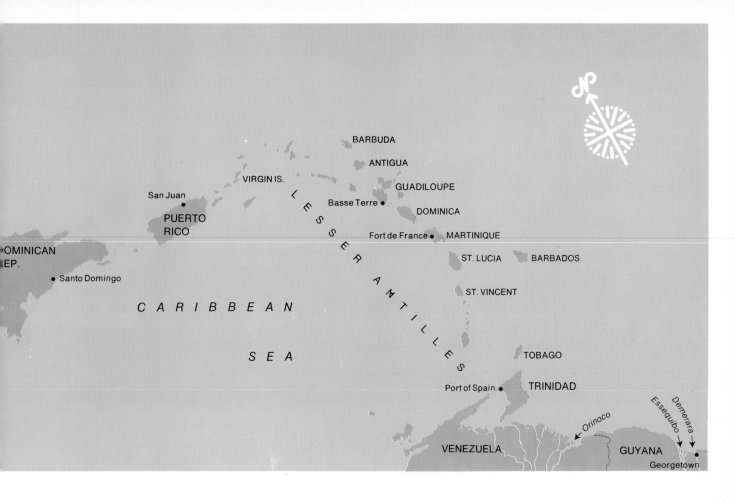

are now making rums lighter in style than of old, to meet modern tastes.

The darkness of most Jamaica and Demerara rums comes partly from ageing but largely from the caramel added to give the colour expected in rich-flavoured rums of this type. The richness of flavour itself is often achieved by the addition of, or by redistillation with, dunder (see above).

But Guyana also produces Imperial White Diamond, a brand as light as the famous Bacardi, which was originally from Cuba and is now distilled by the Bacardi firm in the Bahamas, in Mexico, in Brazil and in Puerto Rico, and is the archetypal light, dry rum. There are medium golden-hued Jamaican rums, too, much less treacly in appearance and in taste than the traditional Jamaican – notably Lemon Hart.

There are light rums from Puerto Rico, too, the island that is perhaps the world's greatest producer of rum, and which dominates the American market (Puerto Rico is United States territory), though a good deal of rum is distilled from imported molasses in New England – the one major rum-producing region in the New World that is not washed by the waters of the Caribbean.

Indeed, New England – particularly Massachusetts, Connecticut and Rhode

Nº 4. Raffinage du Sucre.

Nº 5. Sucre rafiné et mis en pains.

Island – was once a major centre of the rum trade, or rather of the vicious 'New England triangle's' trade in the course of which molasses was imported from the West Indies to be made into rum; the rum was then shipped to West Africa where it paid for slaves who, if they survived the voyage to the Caribbean, filled the ships in which they had been herded more cruelly than cattle with more molasses for New England.

Medford was the centre of the eighteenth-century New England rum trade and gave its name generically to the produce: when Paul Revere, in his own account, recorded that he 'refreshed himself' at Medford in the course of his midnight ride to Lexington, his readers had no doubt as to what with. Rum was indeed a familiar creature to the patriots of 1776: George Washington was already a member of the Virginia House of Burgesses (which sent him to the Continental Congress, thanks to 75

Saint Thomas, 1825. Until 1863 this island, 'the gateway to the Caribbean', was Danish. An important part of the German rum trade is still concentrated in Flensburg, formerly a Danish town.

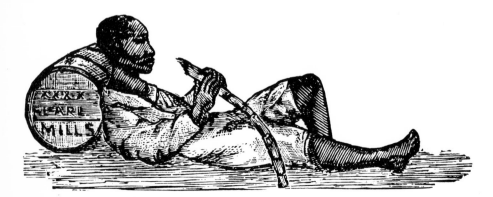

gallons of rum diplomatically distributed among the voters).

And New England resentment at the 1764 renewal of the Sugar Act, penally taxing imported molasses for the rum trade, was as much a contributory cause to the Revolution as the tax on tea.

Thus it figured in American history from before the Declaration of Independence down to the Volstead Act and the Eighteenth Amendment. Not all the liquor shipped illegally during

Prohibition into the United States through French and British West Indian islands was rum (much of it was whisky) but the very name was already so much a part of American folk-lore that the men and the ships that carried it were at once named and known as rum-runners, and the fast speedboats that ran their cargoes in past the Coast Guard cutters waited in Rum Row.

Meanwhile, rum was making its impression on the French national consciousness, too – but, characteristically, in the cookery books rather than the history books.

The *patron-chef*, Raymond Oliver, has stated in his classic of social history, *The French at Table*, that in the seventeenth and the eighteenth centuries rum and ratafia (grape juice the fermentation of which has been checked by the addition of spirit) were the most important alcoholic culinary additives. A Bordelais himself, he quotes the Gascon recipes for roast snipe and for pigeon, which call for red wine and rum.

Bordeaux was and is, of course, the obvious port for the West Indian trade, and it was from Bordeaux, according to Monsieur Oliver, that the custom spread of drinking rum with Dutch cheese. (Dutch cheese is the improbable favourite of the Bordelais who, unlike all the rest of their compatriots, make no serious cheese of their own : the taste for it has been traditional in the region since the days when sailing ships took claret to Rotterdam and came back with the round, hard, heavy Dutch cheeses as ballast.)

It is significant that the greatest French liqueur and rum-importing firm, Bardinet, is at Bordeaux : its Rhum Negrita (also known as 'Old Nick') is much used for cooking and its bottled 'Old Nick' punch is a branded Planter's Punch taken as an aperitif, and based on rum, sugar syrup and lemon.

Left : Part of a map of Martinique. Most of the rum consumed in France comes from this island.

Most of the rum consumed in France is from Martinique, where almost every kind of rum is produced, from light whites to such dark, rich and aromatic rums as Rhum Saint James and such old liqueur rums as the Duquesne Val d'Or.

The distilling of rum was introduced into the French West Indies in the late seventeenth century by the Dominican Father Jean-Baptiste Labat, who introduced the same sort of still as was, and is, used in the Charentes for the production of cognac.

In Haiti, where the French cultural tradition is still strong, the soil also is very similar to that of the Charentes, and fine liqueur rums, such as Rhum Barbancourt, are double-distilled from Charentais-type pot stills.

Not that rum is much drunk as an after-dinner liqueur or digestive, whether in France or Britain or the United States, though I have enjoyed Bacardi Anejo, aged in wood to become bland and smooth, with coffee after dinner, like a good brandy or an old malt whisky. Wherever rum is drunk it is most frequently as a mixer, in long or short, hot or cold drinks. This is not a book of recipes, but mention must be made of at any rate a few typical examples, for rum is much more widely used in this way than whisky or brandy – more even than gin. Hot grogs and toddies are simple enough: rum, hot water and sugar will do. One of the best, though, is made with a little extra care: it is made by the glass, by pouring a tot of dark rum, such as Jamaica, into a half-pint glass mug, adding a tablespoon of lemon juice, about a teaspoon of sugar, and filling up with hot Indian tea, not too strong. Garnish with a twist of lemon peel.

Use hot water instead of tea, put in three or four whole cloves, float a walnut-sized piece of butter on top, stirring it gently until it dissolves, and you have hot buttered rum, which is much admired and enjoyed by some.

The late Julian Street, a great American gourmet and lover of life, had a simple but sound recipe for a hot rum-and-milk – he mixed in a tumbler three tablespoons of rum, a teaspoon of sugar and three or four drops of vanilla essence (it is better still to keep a vanilla pod in a screw-topped jar of sugar, and to use this vanilla sugar, and not essence) and filled with milk that had been heated but not boiled.

This splendid drink is not only a comforting concoction in itself, but has the added merit that it reminded its inventor of the Mark Twain story about the temperance lecturer in the United States who, visiting a dairy-farming district, diplomatically asked for a glass of milk to be placed on his lecture desk instead of the usual water. The local wag seized the opportunity of putting rum in the milk, and when the lecturer, pausing for refreshment, took a deep swig, he looked admiringly at the empty glass as he set it down and murmured, 'Lord, what cows!'

Of the many cold drinks based on rum, one long and one short must suffice. Planter's Punch is a classic, but the recipe is not sacrosanct. The old jingle calls for 'one of sour, two of sweet, three of strong, four of weak' – the sour being lime-juice, the sweet sugar, the strong rum, and the weak ice. The whole lot to be shaken with crushed ice. But there are variants and fancy elaborations.

Hot buttered rum

Planter's Punch

Rum and milk

Daiquiri

Grog

The Daiquiri cocktail consists of three or four parts of white rum to one part of the juice of fresh limes with soft sugar to taste – a small teaspoon is usually about right – shaken vigorously with finely crushed ice and strained into ice-cold cocktail glasses.
(Or, better still, keep the rum in a cold refrigerator and mix in a jug with a separate ice-container, and you do not need to dilute the good creature with crushed ice.)

The Daiquiri had long been a favourite cocktail in a small, closed group in the United States – among those rich Easterners, that is, who habitually spend holidays in the Caribbean, and those already familiar with Graham Greene's *Our Man in Havana* (1958) the characters in which seem sometimes to be afloat in it.
By about 1960, though, it had become as frequent as the Martini in a very much wider middle-class circle. Clearly, this

was because of President Kennedy's known partiality, by then much publicised, like everything else about his and his family's tastes and habits, for a Daiquiri before dinner, though I used to wonder whether there was not also, in those almost obsessively Castro-conscious days, a wistful element of national nostalgia about the fashion: Daiquiri is the place where, in 1898, at the outbreak of the Spanish-American war, the United States Marines landed in Cuba.

The unsweetened Fruit Brandies (Alcools blancs)

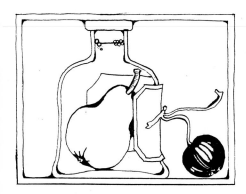

'Eau de Vie' – 'Water of life' – is the general French term for a potable distilled spirit or hard liquor.

In the widest sense, it means 'brandy', though what we usually think and speak of as 'brandy' is, strictly speaking, 'eau de vie de vin', distilled from wine.

But although all brandies made from wine, such as cognac and armagnac, are eaux de vie, not all eaux de vie are made from wine.

By a merciful dispensation of Providence, brandy can be made from fruits, and this chapter concerns itself with fruit brandies.

Not, let me hasten to say, the lusciously sweet, prettily coloured, fruit-*flavoured* liqueurs usually called 'cherry brandy', 'apricot brandy', and the like. These are cordials rather than brandies – sweetened and flavoured liqueurs dealt with in chapter 8.

True brandies, or 'eaux de vie', in the strictest sense, can be made from almost any fruit. There are two principal ways in which this can be done (and, of course, minor, regional variations). In Germany, where many such brandies are made, the distinction is made in the naming of the product. Either the mash of the fruit is allowed to ferment, and alcohol distilled from the mash. In German, this would be a *wasser* – as it might be Kirchwasser, from a mash of cherries, and one of the best-known. The other way is to steep the fruit in alcohol, then to re-distil the spirit thus flavoured. This is the method by which a *geist* is produced – thus,

Himbeergeist, which is distilled from alcohol in which raspberries have been macerated, and the same thing as the French eau de vie de framboise.

In either case, the resultant spirit will be dry, because the sugar of the fruit has been fermented out, and unless it is then aged in casks, taking on colour from the wood, it is as colourless as water – as, indeed, whisky would be, were it not aged in cask and, usually, coloured with caramel. In France, where a great many of the very finest of these fruit brandies come from, they are referred to as 'alcools blancs'.

Then, across the Atlantic, there is the American applejack, neither so good nor so widely drunk as in colonial and revolutionary times (it is usually a blend, these days, of true apple brandy and neutral spirit) and – much more important – the Mexican spirits distilled from the juices of different species of cactus: mescal, from the dumpling cactus, or mescal agave, and tequila, from another variety of agave.

Tequila is said to be the drink of the Mexican middle classes, whereas mescal, which has traces of the hallucinatory drug, mescalin, in it, is the peon's tipple. No doubt the Mexican peon has the greater need to see visions and dream dreams.

There has been something of a vogue for tequila in North America, where it is sometimes used as a basis for mixed drinks and cocktails, but traditionally it is taken neat, in small, very cold, nips like vodka and schnapps.

Tequila, the Mexican eau de vie distilled from agave, is drunk – as tradition requires – after a suck at a slice of lemon and a lick of a pinch of salt.

There is a ritualistic way of taking it after a suck at a slice of lemon and a lick of a pinch of salt placed on the pad of flesh between thumb and forefinger on the back of the hand. Whether it is worth the trouble is a matter for debate...

An exception is calvados, the apple brandy of Normandy – the only one of France's fruit-brandies to be aged in wood, so that it takes on a honey-coloured or a tawny tint. This great drink comes from just beyond the northernmost frontier of Europe's wine-growing region, and other fruit brandies come from outlying parts of it, two of them especially and justly famous – slivovitz, the plum brandy of Yugoslavia and other Balkan countries, and barack palinka, Hungary's potent but highly palatable brandy distilled from fermented apricots and their kernels, and no relation of the sweet apricot brandies referred to in chapter 8.

These apart, virtually all the world's great classic fruit-brandies come from one geographical region: the upper reaches of the Rhine and the high upland country on its either side – from the Swiss countryside between Basle and the river's source in Lake Constance; from the Alsatian plain and the deep valleys of the Vosges on the French side; and from the Black Forest on the German. Some have French names, but rather more have German, as coming either from Germany or from German-speaking parts of France and of Switzerland.

The best-known, perhaps, is the one made originally from the wild black cherry of the region, but increasingly from cultivated cherries of the same sort – the brandy that may be referred to in Germany as Schwarzwalder kirschwasser, as coming from the Black Forest; in Switzerland as Basler kirschwasser, for it comes from near Basle; but in Alsace and the world at large as kirsch, simply, a godsend to fruit salad, and a noble after-dinner drink in its own right.

The cherries for kirsch are fermented, and the resultant mash twice distilled in the same kind of old-fashioned stills in which brandy and malt whisky are made. The fermentation is exactly the same as the fermentation of the juice of grapes for wine, transforming the sugar content of the fruit into alcohol, and the distillation exactly the same process as turns wine into cognac. And the process is basically the same for the other fruits that the Rhinelanders – German, Swiss or Alsatian – make into eaux de vie.

More highly regarded even than kirsch, partly because it is more expensive; more expensive because it takes so much fruit to produce a gallon; and likely to disappear from the market because workers cannot be found to undertake the back-breaking task of gathering the wild fruit, is framboise, made from the wild raspberries of the Vosges – a miraculously paradoxical combination of dryness and fruit, austerity and fragrance.

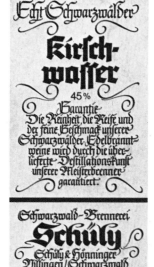

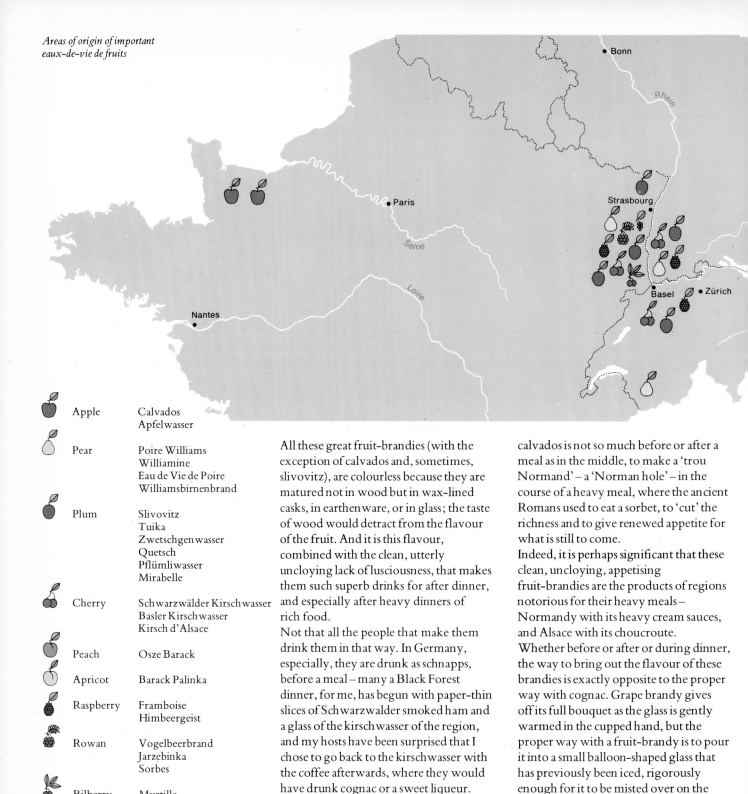

Areas of origin of important
eaux-de-vie de fruits

Apple	Calvados Apfelwasser	
Pear	Poire Williams Williamine Eau de Vie de Poire Williamsbirnenbrand	
Plum	Slivovitz Tuika Zwetschgenwasser Quetsch Pflümliwasser Mirabelle	
Cherry	Schwarzwälder Kirschwasser Basler Kirschwasser Kirsch d'Alsace	
Peach	Osze Barack	
Apricot	Barack Palinka	
Raspberry	Framboise Himbeergeist	
Rowan	Vogelbeerbrand Jarzębinka Sorbes	
Bilberry	Myrtille	
Holly-berry	Baie de houx	

All these great fruit-brandies (with the exception of calvados and, sometimes, slivovitz), are colourless because they are matured not in wood but in wax-lined casks, in earthenware, or in glass; the taste of wood would detract from the flavour of the fruit. And it is this flavour, combined with the clean, utterly uncloying lack of lusciousness, that makes them such superb drinks for after dinner, and especially after heavy dinners of rich food.

Not that all the people that make them drink them in that way. In Germany, especially, they are drunk as schnapps, before a meal – many a Black Forest dinner, for me, has begun with paper-thin slices of Schwarzwalder smoked ham and a glass of the kirschwasser of the region, and my hosts have been surprised that I chose to go back to the kirschwasser with the coffee afterwards, where they would have drunk cognac or a sweet liqueur. And it is different again in Normandy, where the time-honoured way to drink calvados is not so much before or after a meal as in the middle, to make a 'trou Normand' – a 'Norman hole' – in the course of a heavy meal, where the ancient Romans used to eat a sorbet, to 'cut' the richness and to give renewed appetite for what is still to come.

Indeed, it is perhaps significant that these clean, uncloying, appetising fruit-brandies are the products of regions notorious for their heavy meals – Normandy with its heavy cream sauces, and Alsace with its choucroute.

Whether before or after or during dinner, the way to bring out the flavour of these brandies is exactly opposite to the proper way with cognac. Grape brandy gives off its full bouquet as the glass is gently warmed in the cupped hand, but the proper way with a fruit-brandy is to pour it into a small balloon-shaped glass that has previously been iced, rigorously enough for it to be misted over on the outside: to fill the glass only half-full, so that the nose can be dipped into the ethers

Munich •

Donau

Vienna •

• Budapest

Duna

Belgrade •

Dunav

RUBUS FRUTICOSUS L.
Die Brombeere

before drinking : part of the enchantment
of these fruit-brandies is their bouquet.
This does not mean, though, as might be
supposed, that the brandy itself should be
kept in the refrigerator, or even in the
cellar. Fruit-brandies mature and mellow
best at ordinary room temperature – it is
only at the moment of drinking that one
should bring out their fragrance by a
sudden chilling. This is another difference
from cognac – fruit-brandies develop in
bottle, and cognac does not.

The first time I visited Alsace, many years ago, I set out to identify the seventeen different kinds of fruit-brandy that I had been told existed in those parts, and sat in solemn session with a director of the great Dolfi distillery at Strasbourg, not disdaining to taste one fruit-brandy against another as we went first through the list of those made commercially at the distillery itself; than those we had tasted at the hospitable tables of mountain farmers who made them at their homes; then those we had heard of in the region but never actually tasted. Game, set, and match, I am proud to recall, went to the visiting English amateur, who confounded the resident Alsatian professional with news of a fruit-brandy he had never heard of – 'eau de vie de baie de houx', or holly-berry brandy which, at the little mountain-top hotel where I was staying, cost twice as much as framboise because of its fantastic rarity, and was not half so nice. Like many another foolish guest, I had felt obliged to try it because it was the most expensive.

The distiller told me that it must have been the produce of one of the local farmers who still had a licence to distil for his own consumption – a class that is dying out, as new licences are no longer issued – many of whom would distil pretty well anything they could lay their hands on, whether from sheer peasant canniness, from enthusiasm, or from a belief that the good God had meant all

fruits to be distilled into Alsatian eaux
de vie.

Meanwhile, though, we had been tasting
the products of the distillery itself, one
against another – not so wide a range as in
the old days, because there are no peasant
families so hard pressed for a few francs
that their woman and children must go
out and pick the wild fruit – bilberries and
blackberries, sloes and rose-hips – that
used to be made into brandy in sizeable
quantities, and are now made only
privately, if at all.

Mostly – except for the wild raspberry
and, to a far lesser extent, the wild
strawberry, the brandies from which are
becoming fantastically expensive – the
fruit-brandies produced commercially are
made from cultivated orchard fruits or, at
any rate, fruits that can easily be picked,
handled, and packed. But there is still a
fierce local pride in them: a good
Strasbourgeois thinks of cognac as being
made of thin, sour wine, whereas *his*
brandies are made of delicious fruit.

In Alsace itself it is still possible to find
such brandies as myrtille, from the
bilberry; prunelle, from the sloe; sorbes,
from the rowan; mure, from the
blackberry; and many others. There is
even a 'tutti frutti' blend of various fruits
occasionally to be found, but it lacks
character, and is never exported. Dr. Fritz
Hallgarten, one of the great authorities on
German and Alsatian wines and brandies,
opines that it is made only by family
distillers who do not pick or produce
enough fruit to fill each cask with one
fruit only.

But outside the areas of production those
most likely to be found, after kirsch and
framboise (probably from Alsace, perhaps
from Germany or Switzerland), calvados
(from Normandy), and slivovitz (from
Yugoslavia), are two plum brandies, both
probably from Alsace – quetsch, distilled
from the small, purple 'switzen' plum;
and mirabelle, from a sweeter, golden
plum. These have a more subtle, less
emphatic flavour than either kirsch or

*In the Swiss canton of Vaud pears are grown into
bottles to enhance the flavour of the eau de vie de
poires known as Poire Williams, or Williamine.*

framboise, and there are some
connoisseurs who esteem them more
highly for that very reason, with
mirabelle perhaps slightly the more
highly regarded of the two.

I must confess, myself, to a liking for the
much more assertive flavour of the
brandy made from William pears, which I
first came across many years ago in a
restaurant in Hanover, run by Greeks, but
of which the best examples, it is generally

agreed, come from Switzerland,
and are known as Poire Williams, or
Williamine.

If I drank this pear brandy often, it may
well be that I should tire of its emphatic
quality – its fragrance can be quite
overwhelming – and turn to the more
reticent, more subtle, flavours and
fragrances of quetsch and of mirabelle.
But I do not drink it often enough: part of
the charm of all these exquisite essences of
fruit is their infrequency. But only a part.
The rest of it is their intensity: drink
kirsch or quetsch or Williamine after
dinner, and you can smell – even before
you taste – that you have an orchard, a
Black Forest hillside, or a valley of the
Vosges encapsulated in the glass you are
cupping in your hand. Few other drinks
are so evocative.

8 Herb-flavoured Liqueurs

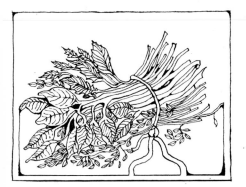

In the direct line of descent from the magic potions and the medicinal infusions concocted by medieval monks and alchemists are the many commercial herb-flavoured liqueurs of our own time, marketed under brand names.

Production now, though, is a good deal more scientific than when bearded self-styled sages threw herbs and who knows what else into a bubbling cauldron and hoped for the best.

Today, there are four main methods by which spirit – whether brandy, whisky, or neutral spirit – is aromatised: distillation, maceration, steeping and percolation.

By the first method, the material, wine or grain-mash, from which the alcoholic spirit is to be derived is distilled *with* the aromatic substances – barks, roots, herbs or fruits.

Some substances such as these lose their fragrance and flavour by this method, and these are macerated or infused – steeped in a cold spirit.

If the solvent spirit is warmed the process is known as steeping or digestion.

The fourth method is percolation, by which the solvent, hot or cold, is trickled or forced through the aromatic substance. All this, of course, is grossly to simplify: serious students are recommended to the books listed in the bibliography, and to a most informative booklet, in Dutch, German, French and English, published by the Amsterdam firm of Bols.

Modern though their methods are, however, all houses that can claim a medieval origin, monastic for preference, do so – and many that cannot, do so all the same.

The archetype herb liqueur, indeed, is Chartreuse, for it is still made by monks, and there is a quasi-medicinal version, peculiar to Chartreuse, the Elixir Végétal, for which are claimed at any rate digestive and tonic qualities, and which is too strong alcoholically to be taken other than in medicinal drops.

The story goes – and it is probably at least as authentic as any of the stories told to publicise the many and varied liqueurs of the same sort – that in 1605 Annibal-François d'Estrées (who had been a bishop at 21 – his sister having become Henri IV's mistress – before he became a Marshal of France) gave to the Carthusian monks of Paris a manuscript formula, devised by some alchemist of any earlier time, for an elixir of long life. It was not until a century and a half later, however, that the Carthusian Brother Jérôme Maubec sorted out the complicated recipe to the point of actually producing the elixir. When he died, in 1762, the brothers were in a position to go on producing both the elixir itself and the less concentrated digestive liquers based upon it.

Production has gone on since then at the monastery of Grande Chartreuse, in the wooded, mountainous sub-Alpine country near Grenoble or, rather, by monks of the monastery in a distillery some twenty-five kilometres away at Voiron. (The product is marketed

The monastery of the Grande Chartreuse.

Carthusian monks still superintend the production of Chartreuse. It is said that only three monks are entrusted with the secret of the 130 herbs from which five concentrated extracts are derived.

by a separate, lay, organisation.) Development must have been gradual at first, and there have been ups and downs. Production went up, for instance, in the eighteen-thirties and eighteen-forties: the elixir was used effectively as a tonic in the cholera epidemic of 1832, and only a few years later Brother Bruno Jacquet produced a rather sweeter, less alcoholically strong version – yellow – of the green liqueur based upon the elixir, and the success of the yellow and the green

was such that a distillery had to be built. In the year of revolutions, 1848, officers of the French Army, billeted on the monastery, were served the liqueur after dinner, and sang its praises in the Paris of the Second Republic and the Second Empire.

There was a set-back in 1901, when the religious orders were expelled from France: the monks established a distillery in Spain, at Tarragona, and although the order returned to France in 1940 it still functions, and three monks from the Grande Chartreuse itself visit it every winter to ensure that the liqueurs made in France and in Spain are identical. These are the three monks who, at any one time, are entrusted with the secret of the 130 herbs from which five concentrated extracts are derived; how each of the five is constituted; and in what proportion they are blended to produce the very strong green Chartreuse, the sweeter and less strong yellow, and the highly concentrated elixir.

Green Chartreuse is one of the most famous liqueurs, one of the most expensive, and one of the strongest. Those who find it too strong taken neat with their after-dinner coffee take the yellow instead or, (say the connoisseurs) a mixture of the two.

Oscar Wilde used to tell the story – and I had it from his son, the late Vyvyan Holland, who wrote the moving *Son of Oscar Wilde*, – of being struck when he visited the Grande Chartreuse by the look

of serene happiness on the faces of the monks. What, he asked the Almoner, was the secret?

'One-third green, two-thirds yellow', said the Almoner.

I have dealt with Chartreuse at some length, partly because of its prestige among herb liqueurs, but chiefly because its story contains elements some or all of which crop up in the background stories of so many other such – the long history;

the aged manuscript; the alchemist and the monks; the secrecy enshrouding the ingredients and their compounding.

La Senancole, for instance, which is not unlike yellow Chartreuse, is made by the Cistercian monks of the Abbey of Senanque, in the south of France; Aiguebelle, also in a strong green and a sweeter yellow version, claims to derive from an ancient manuscript discovered in a monastery – this time Trappist; and with this must be mentioned a liqueur actually called Trappistine, from – it need hardly be said – an ancient formula in the possession of the Abbaye de Grace-Dieu in the Doubs region, not all that far from the Grande Chartreuse, and the strong Grignan, made by Trappists near Ventoux. And in Germany, too, a green and a yellow liqueur, Etaller, is made at the Benedictine Kloster Ettel, near Oberammergau.

To the Carthusians, Cistercians, Benedictines and Trappists we can add the Capuchins, for it is claimed for the sweet, fragrant, Elixir de Spa that its formula was found in what had been a Capuchin friary dissolved during the Revolution. Understandably, all these, and all other similar liqueurs, keep their formulae secret and make no secret of that secrecy: it is part of the commercial picture.

It is claimed for Chartreuse that no fewer than 130 herbs go to its making, but only the three monks already mentioned know which herbs and in what proportions. Other liqueurs claim anything from a couple of dozen to a hundred: indeed, one

Lannion
Elixer d'Amorique

🏛 Fécamp
Bénédictine DOM

Brussels

Rheinberg
Underberg

Wolfenbüttel
Jägermeister

Bonn

Meuse

Spa
Elixer de Spa

Ettelbrück
Elixer de Mondorf

Frankfurt

Seine

Rhein

Amer Picon

Paris

Main

Nantes

Loire

Donau

Fernet Branca
Saint Louis

Munich
Ettaler

Salzburg

🏛 Grâce Dieu
Trappistine

Doubs

Basel

Zürich

Appenzell
Alpenkräuter

Berchtesgaden
*Alpenkräuter
Enzian*

*Cordial Médoc
La Vieille Cure*
Bordeaux 🏛 Cenon

Saône

Lyon

Aiguebelle
Notre Dame d'Aiguebelle

*Centerbe
Mentuccia*

Millefiori
Saronno

Dordogne

Garonne

Voiron 🏛
Chartreuse

Grenoble

Milan
*Campari
Fernet Branca
Fior d'Alpe*

Adige

Verona
Sambuca

Venice
Galliano

Bayonne
Izarra

Rhône

*Elixer de
Monbazillac*

Turin

Po

Toulouse

🏛 Ventoux
Grignan

Ferrara

Avignon
Elixer du Mont Ventoux

🏛 Senanque
La Sénancole

Genoa

Bologna
Pelinkovac

Nice

Tiber

Rome

Strega
Benevento

Napels

Production areas of herb-flavoured liqueurs

🏛 Liqueurs produced in monasteries

Italian liqueur is called Centerbe, to proclaim that it calls upon the flavours of a hundred herbs, no less, though it is notably mint-flavoured (it is also called Mentuccia) whereas most liqueurs of the Chartreuse type blend their informing flavours in such a way that none predominates.

None of the liqueurs so far mentioned in this chapter names its alcoholic base, which one must assume to be a neutral spirit, but there are those that do : Vieille Cure, for instance, which claims, almost as a matter of course, to be produced according to an ancient recipe from the Abbey of Cenon, (and is put up in a bottle in the shape of a Gothic arch, with a stained-glass-window design for a label) is based on a blend of brandies – both cognac and armagnac. Another liqueur from the same region, the Gironde, Cordial-Médoc, is also based upon brandy, and is flavoured not only with herbs but with fruits.

Izarra, of which, like Chartreuse, there are green (stronger) and yellow (sweeter) versions, is informed with the flavour of herbs and flowers and based upon honey and 'the finest brandies of the south west' – one hopes both cognac and armagnac, for it is produced at Bayonne, in the Basque country, (Izarra is the Basque word for 'star') between the two great brandy-producing regions. It is very reminiscent of Chartreuse.

One of the best-known, highly-regarded and widely-imitated of French herb liqueurs, Bénédictine, is also based upon brandy : in recent years, the proprietor firm has bought no fewer than four old cognac houses – Dor, Commandon, Gautier and Favraud – to ensure supplies of the essential spirit.

Bénédictine, too, makes much of its monkish origins. It is the only brand-named liqueur other than Chartreuse to be mentioned by name in the great litany of liqueurs in that 'breviary of decadence', J.K. Huysmans's

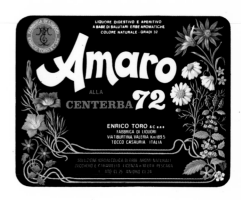

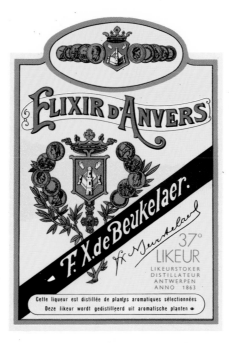

A Rebours, in which we find Des Esseintes gazing at 'the squat, dark-green bottle, which normally conjured up visions of medieval priories for him, with its antique monkish paunch, its head and neck wrapped in a parchment cowl, its red seal quartered with three silver mitres... its label inscribed in sonorous Latin, on paper apparently yellowed and faded with age : Liquor Monachorum Benedictinorum Abbatiae Fiscanensis.

'Under this truly monastic habit, certified

A poster of 1898 by Lopez Silva with the Bénédictine monastery of Fécamp in the background.

by a cross and the ecclesiastical initials D.O.M.,... there slumbered a saffron-coloured liqueur of exquisite delicacy. It gave off a subtle aroma of angelica and hyssop mixed with seaweed whose iodine and bromine content was masked with sugar: it stimulated the palate with a spirituous fire hidden under an altogether virginal sweetness...'
And Des Esseintes dreams over 'the extraordinary discrepancy... between the liturgical form of the bottle and the utterly feminine, utterly modern soul inside it.'

'Utterly modern', indeed. Bénédictine had been produced commercially for only a dozen years or so before *A Rebours* was published, in 1882, and by a layman, elaborate though its claim to derive from a formula of the sixteenth century, and the grandiose monastic form of its present headquarters in Normandy.

An interesting variant is the liqueur B and B – the same strength as Bénédictine and with much the same flavour, but drier because it is half Bénédictine and half brandy. The odd thing is that it was first made for the American market, which is generally supposed to have a sweeter tooth than the British or the French. Some years ago, American bartenders and wine-waiters were reporting that customers were asking for half-and-half brandy and Bénédictine – a mixture becoming so well-known as to be instantly comprehended if called for as 'a B-and-B.' Some devotees of the mixture complained that too often the poorest sort

98

of Californian brandy was used, and so the Bénédictine people decided to do the barman a good turn by providing the mixture ready bottled (a good turn, that is, unless it cut his profit), the customer a good turn by using decent – though quite young – cognac, and themselves a good turn by making a profit on the whole drink instead of only on half of it. Thus a very agreeable new after-dinner liqueur was created, and a useful principle established: any herb or fruit liqueur will retain its flavour whilst losing a great deal of its sticky sweetness by being 'cut' half-and-half with its basic spirit – apricot brandy with brandy; Drambuie, of which more anon, with Scotch whisky, and Irish Mist with Irish.

Italians and others make herb liqueurs very similar to those of France but with little or no insistence upon the Church as a mother. It must be supposed that Mother Church would have frowned, in fact, upon Strega, a liqueur rather like Bénédictine, from the wild,

Izarra and Bénédictine are herbal liqueurs with a brandy base. A variant of Bénédictine is B & B, half Bénédictine and half brandy.

Mint, gentian and coriander are important herbs used – with many others – in the very old and very secret recipes of monastic origin. Gentian is a main ingredient in liqueurs such as Alpenkräuter, Fleur des Alpes and Millefiori.

superstition-ridden mountain country around Benevento, in Central Italy, for the name itself means 'witch' and legend has it that it began as a magic compound that united for ever the man and woman who drank it together – which would leave those of us who have lived in Italy with a heavy load of commitments: I cannot even remember their names... But there are far more bizarre, macabre and outlandish names than Strega on the bottles of Italian herb liqueurs: Battleaxe,

for instance, boldly labelled as such in English, and Latte di Suocèra, 'mother-in-law's milk', with a skull and crossbones on the label. Pelinkovac owes its un-Italian name to the fact that its maker-inventor is a Slav from what used to be Italian territory, now Yugoslav, on the eastern coast of the Adriatic. He now lives and works in Bologna but imports his herbs from his native heath, blending a distillation of them with a local red wine to make a deep brown liqueur with a

marked herby bitterness underlying the sweetness.
Less out of the ordinary than any of these names, but still eschewing claims to any ancient monastic origin, is that of the Italian herb liqueur best-known in the United States – Galliano, named after an Italian hero of the otherwise inglorious Abyssinian campaign of 1895–6: a picture of the fort that Major Galliano defended against overwhelming odds is on every label, but the tall, slender, conical bottle

is boxed in a carton that bears a picture of a carabiniere in full fig.

Attractive or intriguing labelling and packaging are a feature of this world of sweet, herb-flavoured liqueurs. Most of the liqueurs themselves are very good; many are very similar; if one is obliged to say (and especially as their respective compositions are secret) that choice between them is a matter of taste then it must also be added that appeal to the eye may be as potent a factor as appeal to the palate. Few bottles, for instance, are so fetching as those – tall and conical, like that of Galliano – that have a long twig inside hung with gleaming white crystals. These are formed by bottling the liqueur, in which a great deal of sugar is in suspension, whilst it is warm: the sugar crystallises as the liqueur cools. There are many brands, under such names as Fior d'Alpi and Fleur des Alpes, compounded of Alpine herbs and flowers: a notable name is that of Millefiori, the 'thousand

The Galliano label with picture of the fort, and carton with carabiniere.

Crème de menthe is usually drunk 'frappé' – on crushed ice – and through a straw.

flowers' of which make Chartreuse, with its mere 130 herbs, seem grudging, and the sweet Spanish Cuarenta-y-Tres – forty-three – which is like yellow Chartreuse, positively parsimonious. Although, as will have been seen, France and Italy, wine-producing countries, dominate the world of liqueurs, because of the enormous variety of their products and also because of the prestige enjoyed by the leading brands, these products are not always or necessarily based upon a spirit derived from wine – brandy, that is. Some non-wine-producing countries, such as Holland and Belgium and England, import French brandy to make liqueurs of their own, and Scotland and Ireland base admirable herb liqueurs each on its own whisky.

Here, legends of old, unhappy far-off things and battles long ago replace the pious myths of France as background stories for the adverstising copywriters to bite on.

Drambuie, best-known of the three or four liqueurs based on Scotch whisky, is said to be the largest-selling liqueur of any kind in the United Kingdom, and the largest-selling imported liqueur in the United States. It is also said – and this is less capable of proof or of disproof – to be made to a recipe given by Bonnie Prince Charlie after his defeat at Culloden in 1746 when, fleeing for his life, he sheltered with a Mackinnon on the Isle of Skye.

Sambuca con mosche or 'with flies'. The 'flies' are coffee beans floated on top of the liqueur.

who, a couple of centuries before, had borne arms for the Empress Maria Theresa.

Some, however good of their kind, are little-known, such as the King's Ginger Liqueur, compounded in Holland for the time-honoured London firm of Berry Brothers. This heart-warming cordial has a better authenticated history than most: it was produced at the turn of the century for the elderly King Edward VII, whose physicians prescribed a warming cordial to be taken when he came back from his drives in the horseless – and roofless – motor-carriages of the time. The dark red Jägermeister and the various gentian-flavoured liqueurs of Bavaria are seldom found outside their own country.

Other single-flavoured liqueurs are among the best-known and most admired. There are many brands, for instance, of mint and peppermint liqueur, some colourless, some a bright green – a colour refreshing in itself. Unlike most liqueurs, the vividly coloured crème de menthe is usually drunk *frappé* – on crushed ice – and through a straw.

There is a ritual, too, about the Italian Sambuca, flavoured with a herb very similar to aniseed, and traditionally served '*con mosche*' – 'with flies', the 'flies' being three coffee beans floating on the top of the glass, either already roasted, or roasted by applying a flame to the surface of the liqueur.

Aniseed itself, like mint, possesses digestive properties and is the informing flavour of a great range of anis and aniseed liqueurs from every liqueur-producing country.

Probably even more effective than liqueurs such as these as a digestive is caraway, for we first meet it, as infants, in the medicinal 'gripe water' prescribed for babies, based on a rectified spirit and flavoured with caraway.

It is still made in Scotland – the name is a contraction of the Gaelic 'an dram Buidheach', 'the drink that satisfies' – from herbs and honey and is none the worse for being 'cut' half-and-half with the Scotch whisky that is its base. So, too, with the similar but perhaps not quite so richly sweet Glen Mist, also a herb-and-Scotch-whisky liqueur, as is Glayva.
Irish Mist, based on Irish whiskey, herbs and heather honey, is deeper in colour and

smokier and stronger in flavour than Drambuie but similar in style and, like Drambuie, goes back to a romantic past in its advertising – back to the Gaels who drank heather-wine before battle with the Danish invaders, then to the 'Wild Geese' – the Irishmen who fled throughout the eighteenth century from the English oppressor to serve in the armies of Europe. The present recipe is said to have been brought from Vienna to Ireland in 1948, saved from the papers of an Irishman

Its more robust, grown-ups' version is kummel, based on caraway or on its near relative, cumin, and made as widely as the aniseed liqueurs, though it is associated more with the Baltic, Scandinavian and Slav countries, along with Holland and Germany, than with milder, Mediterranean climes.

One version, Danziger Goldwasser, originally made in Danzig, but now in Western Germany, adds aniseed to caraway and, more spectacularly, flecks of real gold leaf. These add nothing to flavour or, one assumes, to the liqueur's digestive properties but they look splendid and bring one back again to the supposedly benign magical qualities of the earliest herb liqueurs: medieval works on the primitive chemistry of the time prescribe gold as a cure-all, and Chaucer, in his 'Canterbury Tales', affirmed that 'gold in physic is a cordial'.

It is the custom to serve these sweet herb liqueurs, and the fruit liqueurs of the following chapter, in tiny 'liqueur glasses', filled to the brim. This seems to me a pity: they smell as pretty as they look, and if the same amount is served in one of the small brandy glasses recommended in chapter 3 there is room to dip the grateful nose into the aromatic ethers…

Finally, although this chapter is about sweet herb liqueurs, mention must be made of alcoholic herbal compounds that are specifically bitter.

Some are so strong and so bitter that they can only be used by the few drops as a flavouring or a colouring – Angostura, for instance. Others with a dash of soda, or with gin, are sweet enough, as well as bitter, to make pleasant aperitifs: Campari is a good example. So, too, are German Stonsdorfer and the Italian Cynar, based not on a herb but on an essence of artichokes, but mentioned here because it is drunk as Campari is, with a splash of soda and a slice of lemon or orange – much enjoyed in France and, they tell me, by Brazilians with gall-bladder trouble.

Most, though, are sold specifically as pick-me-ups, especially as cures for morning-after headaches and hangovers. Amongst their number are the French Amer Picon, the German Underberg, and the Italian Fernet Branca. Their effectiveness as such cannot be doubted: no one would drink them for fun …

Of all bitters Campari is undoubtedly the best-known. Poster by Enrico Sacchetti, 1921.

9 Sweet Fruit Liqueurs or Cordials

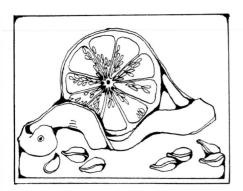

It may well be that in the Middle Ages, once the art of distilling ardent spirits became generally known, housewives found that summer fruits could be preserved for winter eating by bottling them in alcohol.

From that, it would be a short step to colouring and flavouring the alcohol by pricking the skins of the fruit, and drinking the liquid as well as eating the solid.

This is a possibility – even a probability – but the real origin of sweet fruit-flavoured liqueurs as we know them to-day seems to date from no longer ago than the late sixteenth or early seventeenth century. The Dutch, who had already played a major part in developing the French cognac trade, by creating the demand for it, organising the production, and even getting the French to grow the right grapes for it, began to ship the dried peel of bitter oranges from their Caribbean island of Curaçao with which to flavour the younger and harsher brandies they imported.

It was an auspicious beginning, for citrus fruits and, especially, their peel blend well with brandy or other spirits, sweetened, to make liquid after-dinner sweetmeats.

(It is as well here to distinguish between the sweet, rich liqueurs *flavoured with* fruits, and the dry, alcoholically stronger eaux de vie *distilled from* fruits, discussed in chapter 7. English and, in general, European usage can be misleading, for the sweet liqueur made by flavouring brandy or neutral spirit with cherries, for instance, is known as 'cherry brandy', whereas the true dry, colourless brandy distilled from cherries is kirsch, or kirschwasser, or eau de vie des cerises. American usage is more precise: it refers to the latter as a fruit brandy, to the former as a cordial. What we are discussing here is what an American would refer to as cordials.)

Curaçao has become a generic name for all orange-flavoured liqueurs, whether colourless; orange-coloured, naturally or artificially, to remind the drinker of its origin; or even coloured by a tasteless vegetable dye to a bright green or a deep blue, presumably to make pretty mixed drinks with.

True to the national tradition, every Dutch distilling firm makes Curaçao, usually in various styles – colourless, coloured, and perhaps in stronger or weaker, less or more pungent, styles. The house of de Kuyper, to take just one example, makes a colourless, a green and a blue Curaçao; an orange-coloured version, called Orange Curaçao, which is rather more bitter in flavour; a so-called Half-and-Half, which is half Curaçao and half orange bitters; a colourless Triple Sec – a name that used to denote an extra distillation and a drier finish and in this case is in fact rather drier and stronger than the others; and a Vieille Maison, orange in colour, based on brandy and not, as are the others, on neutral spirit. Most other distilleries make a similar range.

The same house revived, in 1952, a liqueur that had appeared three hundred years earlier, at a banquet to celebrate the Dutch landing at the Cape of Good Hope: it is strong, based partly on herbs as well as on the peel of sweet and bitter oranges, and named Pimpeltjens. Although it has now been marketed, in its present-day form, for a quarter of a century, it is still so little-known, even in its native country, that in 1975 the officer of Dutch customs at Rotterdam airport told me that he had never heard of it. All the same, it deserves its mention here for, if it was drunk at or in celebration of the Dutch landing at the Cape, it is the spiritual ancestor of the notable South African liqueur, also based on herbs and a citrus fruit, the South African naartjes, a sort of tangerine, and called Van der Hum, which is as much to say, 'Mr What's-his-Name.'

Every country that produces citrus fruit – and many that merely import them –

108

makes citrus-flavoured liqueurs, from the Greek Kitro, the Turkish Portakal, the Italian Aurum and the Corfiote liqueur made from the tiny Japanese-type cumquat oranges, by way of Cyprus, Israel, and the Belgian and the Danish Mandarine, to the American Forbidden Fruit, based partly on the shaddock, a type of grape-fruit, partly on honey and orange, and presented in the most ornate of all liqueur bottles, shaped and decorated like the orb of royal regalia.

Two French commercial brands, however, clearly typify different styles of orange-flavoured liqueur. Grand Marnier is cognac-based and a deep gold in colour: it uses the peel only of bitter oranges. Cointreau is colourless, based on a neutral spirit, and uses sweet as well as bitter orange-peel.
Both are fine after-dinner drinks and deserve their world fame, but the Grand Marnier is subtler and deeper in flavour, the Cointreau lighter and less lusciously cloying.
Cointreau used to be called simply Triple Sec, but that term is now used by almost every firm for its colourless version of Curaçao, and Cointreau relies now simply on the name of its founding family.
Parfait Amour, made by both French and Dutch distillers, is said to be based on citrus oils, but is coloured, scented and flavoured to resemble a sweet essence of violets. Elderly roués used to lavish it, at the end of purposeful little dinners, on impressionable young ladies. Nowadays, young ladies are not so easily impressed...

After the citrus fruits, cherries and apricots are probably the fruits most widely used in the making of sweet liqueurs.
Again, pretty well every country that makes liqueurs at all makes cherry brandy, but there are two main types – the colourless Maraschino, originally from the Dalmatian coast of the Adriatic, which is now Yugoslav, but now chiefly from Italy, and the richly red cherry

Two world-famous French orange-flavoured liqueurs: Grand Marnier and Cointreau.

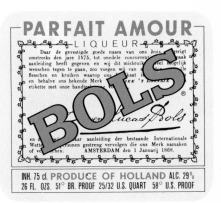

109

brandies from further north: France's
Rocher cherry brandy, for instance,
Denmark's Cherry Heering, and Grant's
Morella Cherry Brandy from the English
cherry-growing county of Kent.
('Kent, sir – everybody knows Kent', says
Mr Jingle in *The Pickwick Papers* – 'apples,
cherries, hops and women.')
No doubt there are modern short cuts,
but basically the very finest cherry
brandies are still made by using fresh fruit
– no essences or preserved fruit – crushing

Cherry orchard in Kent. The finest cherry brandies
are made by using fresh fruit.

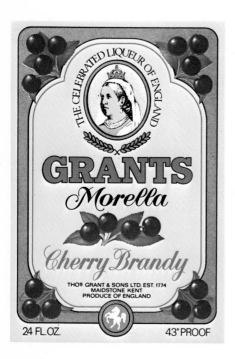

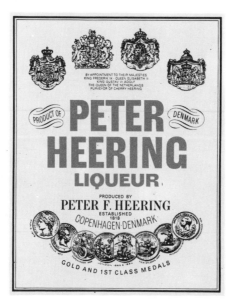

the stones and the fruit separately and
steeping them with sugar in young French
brandy.
It is only a dozen years ago that I saw the
process being carried out in a distillery in
one of the oldest parts of Rotterdam,
across a narrow canal from the church
where the Pilgrim Fathers worshipped
before returning across the North Sea in
the *Speedwell* to join the *Mayflower*.
It was in the same old distillery that I saw
apricot brandy being made. To my mind

(or, rather, to my palate) apricots seem to preserve their integrity of flavour more intensely in liqueur form than any other fruit, including cherries.

Both fresh and dried apricots were used, some from Holland but some from as far away as California : again both the fruit and the stones were crushed, but added to the young brandy was a spirit ('the ghost of the apricot') distilled from the dried fruit, to intensify the taste.

All liqueur-manufacturers produce apricot brandies, some of course better than others. Mixed half-and-half with brandy the very best show a much drier 'finish' without any noticeable diminution of the taste of apricot. Mention of mixtures is a reminder that an English magazine, the *Field,* devoted to shooting, fishing and fox-hunting, recently commended as the best drink which to fill a hunting-flask a mixture of whisky and cherry brandy known as a Percy Special, after a famous North-country pack.

(Some firms compound cherry whiskies, but they have never been even remotely so popular as cherry brandies.)
No doubt the greater the proportion of whisky the more effective as what our grandfathers used to call a 'jumping powder', though I have been told by the head of one of London's most ancient wine merchants that this was more usually 'some sort of blackstrap port', and the novelist, Robert Smith Surtees, who hunted somewhere near the Percy country in early-Victorian times, filled John Jorrocks's hunting-flask with brandy.

Sloe gin, made by steeping sloes in sweetened gin, is a particularly English liqueur – Hawkers' Pedlar brand is at any rate nationally famous – and the other cordial traditionally at home in the hunting-field. All these stirrup cups – cherry brandy, cherry whisky and sloe gin – make good after-dinner drinks, too, which is more than can be said for what

the millionaire Nubar Gulbenkian once told an anti-blood-sport spectator he was swigging from his cavernous silver flask : port wine and fox's blood.

It will have been noted that both cherry and apricot brandies owe some of their flavour to the stones as well as the fruit. A few liqueurs are made of fruit-stones alone : the best-known is crème de noyau, perhaps the finest of which is the Veuve Champion Noyau Rosé, now made in Bordeaux but from a Martinique recipe. It is the palest possible pink, made from the essences of both peach and apricot kernels, and tastes of almonds. Although peaches do not have the same pungency as apricots, Pêche is well-known in France and one of the finest and most famous of all liqueurs, the American Southern Comfort, originally from New Orleans, is made principally from peaches (discernible to the nose) along with herbs and oranges, with a base of old Bourbon whisky.

Advertisement for Southern Comfort, a fruit liqueur on a base of old Bourbon, originally from New Orleans.

Commissioned in 1974 to devise a drink to commemorate the release of the film *The Great Gatsby,* and the reissue by Penguin Books of Scott Fitzgerald's novel itself, I felt that there ought to be a truly American ingredient and proposed Southern Comfort. Bitters were needed to cut the sweetness a little, and as Southern Comfort is based on peaches as well as Bourbon it seemed proper that they should be peach bitters. Penguin Books insisted that there should be champagne in it, for the book – and Gatsby, and Scott Fitzgerald in his time – was full of it, and so as printed in the invitation to the publication party the recipe for Fizz-Gerald (it was thus that in the euphoria occasioned by the preliminary tastings I dubbed it) read as follows:

'Into an eight-ounce wine glass put one thick slice of orange and drop on to it 6–8 drops of peach bitters. Add one jigger (about an ounce and a half) of Southern Comfort and fill the glass with champagne'.

By the end of the publication party the prettiest guest was under a table – and not without companionship.

There are as many fruit liqueurs as there are fruits, and it is impossible to mention them all: it would need a book as big as Britannica. Faraway Finland, for instance, makes deliciously bitter-sweet liqueurs of the fragrant small berries of the sub-Arctic north – Karpi, from cranberries, Lakka from cloudberries, and Mesimarja from the hardy blackberries of the region.

For the last place in this unavoidably sketchy chapter, crème de cassis nominates itself, not merely because of its enticing colour and intensity of blackcurrant flavour but because it, too, is an immensely helpful mixer – much more so, indeed, even than Southern Comfort.

Strong as it is – not far short of the potency of Green Chartreuse – it is sweet and smooth in the mouth, but not so sugary as the liqueurs based on Scotch whisky, such as Drambuie, and with a noticeably drier finish.
Most European drinkers consider it an after-dinner digestive, but many Americans use it as a base for various mixed drinks, substituting it for straight Bourbon or rye in such whisky cocktails as a Manhattan.

Blackcurrant liqueurs are very widely made, but the classic home of crème de cassis is Dijon, the capital of Burgundy and thus a great gastronomic centre, famous for its mustard, its snails, its wine – and its blackcurrants.

An excellent digestive after-dinner liqueur in its own right, cassis (as it is usually referred to, but it must not be confused with the dry white wine of Cassis on the Mediterranean coast) is mixed with champagne (champagne-cassis) dry vermouth (vermouth-cassis) and cognac (cognac-cassis or 'cassisco') to say nothing of the various proprietary aperitifs such as Byrrh, Dubonnet and the rest.

It is most widely-used, though, as a mixer with any fairly ordinary local dry white wine, such as a Bourgogne Aligoté, to which it gives a pretty colour, a touch of sweetness, and a deliciously fruity taste – the wine giving dryness and a refreshing acidity. This mixture is so much an everyday speciality of the region that is used to be called *rince cochon* or pig-rinse, until it was remarked that it was the favourite aperitif and between-the-meals drink of Canon Kir, the stubbornly patriotic mayor of Dijon during the German occupation, and a sturdily left-wing local politician after it. Since his time, the mixture has been *un kir*: men have had worse memorials.

Peace to his ashes – and a suitable libation …

This painting by Kees van Dongen was reproduced on the cover of the reissue by Penguin books of Scott Fitzgerald's The Great Gatsby. *For the publication party a cocktail 'Fizz Gerald' was invented by the author of this book, based on Southern Comfort and champagne.*

Tea, Cocoa and more especially Coffee

I lived for a time in Cognac, working on a book about that tiny country town's supremely noble product.

Making the acquaintance of the splendid brandy's cousins and in-laws – such liqueurs, for instance, as Grand Marnier and Bénédictine, discussed in previous chapters – I came across Sève Patricia, a Sève liqueur based on cognac, as other Sèves have other bases.

To my surprise, I found that among the herbs employed in its flavouring, along with fruits and sugar, was tea.

I should not have been so taken aback – no Englishman should be taken aback to find tea in unlikely places, for the English have taken it to the unlikeliest – for tea is not only a delicately flavoured herb (I suppose it *is* a herb: what else?) but can enhance other flavours.

And if tea is to be classed as a herb, then tea liqueurs should perhaps have been discussed in chapter 8. But there appear to be few of them – there used to be a French 'Tea Breeze', made by Marie Brizard, but it seems to have disappeared, and although I have heard of the Japanese Green Tea Liqueur, based on brandy, I have never tasted it.

I mention tea here, though, as an introduction to two other beverages, cocoa and coffee, made not from leaves but from beans, and beans that have a special place in any account of liqueurs. The cocoa bean and its chocolate derivative lend themselves particularly well to the making of rich, sweet liqueurs: virtually every major liqueur manufacturer lists a crème de cacao, under that or some other name, many of them flavoured, as are so many chocolate bars and bonbons, with vanilla.

Chocolate lends itself, too, to blending with other flavours: there is a German nut-chocolate liqueur; Bailey's Irish Cream blends chocolate with cream and Irish whiskey; and one of the most interesting and successful innovations in the world of liqueurs dates from no longer ago than 1963 when Peter Hallgarten, then only in his thirties, compounded his Royal Mint-Chocolate Liqueur, devised in London but produced now in France to his secret formula. It reproduces in liquid form the flavour of the after-dinner mint-chocolate sweetmeat that had recently become, and remains, so widely popular.

It is natural enough, perhaps, that coffee should play an even bigger part than cocoa in the world of after-dinner liqueurs, just as coffee is so much more universally acceptable as an after-dinner drink than cocoa is.

It is not only the coffee-producing countries that produce coffee liqueurs – all countries that make liqueurs, from Scotland to Turkey, import the beans or the essences to make them, and the firm of Heering, for instance, makes the Mexican Kahlua in Denmark under licence.

Vienna has been famous for its coffee and its cafés since 1684, when Franz Kolschitzky, a successful spy, was

There are variants. I have had it made with the herb liqueur Irish Mist (see chapter 10) at the house of the man who produces it – made in precisely the same way as Irish coffee, but with no need for sugar, and offering an additional subtle taste of herbs. Use Scotch whisky instead of Irish and it is called Highland coffee, and when brandy has been used I have heard it called Gaelic coffee, though what the Gaels have to do with brandy I do not know – unless it consoles them for

rewarded by the grateful Austrians with bags of coffee-beans left behind by the Turks after raising their siege, and opened a coffee-house by St. Stephen's Cathedral. It is surprising, therefore, that there seems to have been no Viennese coffee liqueur until about 1960, when 'Old Vienna' coffee brandy was launched, made by Meinl, a firm famous in the city for its coffees, and blended with French brandy. It has a stronger flavour of coffee than Kahlua, which is less alcoholically strong, and than the famous Tia Maria, based on Jamaican rum and extracts of Blue Mountain coffee, but with a hint of vanilla in its complex flavour.

Gallwey's Irish Coffee Liqueur, made in Waterford of Irish whiskey, honey, herbs and coffee essence, although bland and sweet, as are all such after-dinner drinks, is not so cloying as Tia Maria and Kahlua, and nearer in strength and style to Old Vienna.

It is not to be confused with Irish coffee, which seems to have swept the restaurants of the sophisticated Western world in a mere generation. As it depends upon a spirit, it has a place in this book, and as it is combined with coffee to make a post-prandial beverage-cum-liqueur, perhaps it is proper that that place should be at the end.

This is the way it is made.

In a heated glass (tall, and preferably with a stem, for this is a hot drink) put an Irish measure, which is two and a half ounces, of Irish whiskey, with sugar to taste. Fill with strong, hot, black coffee to within about an inch of the brim. Stir thoroughly.

Then pour double cream on to the surface, very gently so that it does not mix – pouring it slowly over the back of a spoon is the best method. The object is to be able to drink the strong, sweet, hot black-coffee-and-whiskey-and-sugar through, with, and in contrast to, the cold, bland, blond cream. This is why it is essential that the stirring be done before the cream is added.

being Gaels. Or unless it was originally not 'Gaelic' but 'Gallic'.

What the brandy mixture ought to be called is 'Gloria', for I have an English cookery book of 1845, Eliza Acton's *Modern Cookery*, which gives a recipe for 'Burnt Coffee, or Coffee à la Militaire (in France vulgarly called Gloria)' which involves pouring brandy gently, over a spoon on to the top of a cup of strong, sweet, black coffee, lighting the brandy 'and when the spirit is in part consumed, blow out the flame, and drink the *gloria* quite hot.'

So the idea of mixing spirits with coffee is by no means new, but the comforting concoction in its Irish form has become so widely known, and done so much in recent years for Irish distilleries that in the middle nineteen-sixties the Irish Government's Department of External Affairs actually devoted a page of its official fortnightly *Bulletin* to discussing its origin, in the same way as the Norwegian Foreign Office pronounced on the proper way to serve aquavit, and as though the U.S. State Department issued a scholarly statement on Martinis. According to this official pronunciamento it was one Joe Sheridan, the then chef at the Shannon Airport restaurant who, in the late nineteen-thirties, hit upon the idea of serving a group of belated and benighted Americans, cold and tired, with hot coffee laced with his native whiskey and topped with his native cream.

The *Bulletin* admits that the notion may well not have been entirely original, but this time it was written about so enthusiastically by a journalist on the *San Francisco Chronicle* that it was taken up as a speciality of the house by a San Francisco restaurant, whence the cult spread along the western seaboard of the United States before crossing the continent to New York. And it was by way of New York that the fashion for this Irish warmer of the cockles of the heart came back to Europe from California – rather as vodka returned to the Old World.

And it is good to see any government department of any nation writing so rhapsodically about anything as the Irish Republic's Department of External Affairs on 'the creative spirit of Joe Sheridan, whose deep compassion for his fellow-human beings, his artist's eye and gourmet's palate fused on that cold wintry night in the late 'thirties by "the dark mutinous waves of the Shannon".' It seems to be the whiskey itself speaking...

Strong coffee and Irish whiskey crowned with lightly whipped cream make Irish coffee a heart-warmer, famous all over the Western world.

Epilogue

The water wagon is the place for me
At twelve o'clock I felt immense,
Today I favour total abstinence,
My eyes are bleared and red and hot,
I ought to eat but I cannot;
It is no time for mirth and laughter –
The cold grey dawn of the morning after...

... which is a song from an American musical comedy of the beginning of the century.

For those in so sad a condition, when the Remembrance of Things Past follows one around like a personal black thundercloud, Byron would have prescribed a hock-and-seltzer, a mawkish mixture; other gentlemen of the period scraped the fur from their matutinal tongues with those instruments of silver on elegantly turned ivory handles still to be found in collections of Georgian silver, and known as tongue-scrapers.
In the hock country itself they take raw herring, onions and sour cream on the morning after, a specific too heroic for me. Nor do I take any more kindly to another old tosspot's tip – a glass of cold milk on going to bed and another on rising. I am not a calf.

There are those who swear by a hair of the dog, and who breakfast on bottled beer and aspirin; some will have nothing but champagne; others speak highly, if in a hoarse voice, of absinthe.
This must be based on some sort of sympathetic magic, or on the principle of strong devils driving out weaker devils, but I have my doubts: you don't treat arsenic poisoning by administering more arsenic, so why try to cure alcohol poisoning by taking more alcohol? Though I have known a Horse's Neck, which is brandy and ginger ale, bring round a sorely afflicted destroyer captain, not only hungover but being fired upon by the King's enemies, to the belief that he would live, and his ship float.

There was an eighteenth-century Surfeit Water that contained twenty-one different herbs and was 'used successfully against cholicks, gripings in the stomach and bowels, flatulencies and vapours, all of which it discusses by its carminative virtue; it attenuates the humours, and helps perspiration and ... expels the malignity from the centre to the circumference, which it discharges by a gentle dew upon the surface of the cuticle'.
This is to sweat it out, and upon the same principle a Turkish or a sauna bath is many a repentant imbiber's first thought.

Opening the pores may be the reason, too, for all those various pick-me-ups based on Worcester sauce, such as the Prairie Oyster, which is the raw yolk of an egg slipped unbroken into a glass containing a tablespoon of Worcester sauce, with a dash of sherry and a touch of red pepper. To my mind, anyone who can even think of the raw yolk of an egg cannot really be hungover.

Prevention is better than cure, especially if the cure is the one used upon habitual drunkards in the New York of the eighteen nineties, to whom specially selected leeches were applied – creatures said to be normally teetotal but which took to drink through the patients' blood, which they sucked, much to the patients' relief, until they themselves fell stupefied to the ground.

So, if prevention is our aim, let us remember the young lady who shyly asked her doctor for an infallible method of contraception. 'Nothing could be simpler', he said: 'just a glass of cold water, my dear'.
The lady was surprised, but was prepared to accept the advice – if only the method was made clear. 'But do tell me,' she said: 'is it to be taken, er – before, or – ahem – after? It could hardly' (she blushed) 'be taken during...'
'No, no', said the doctor: 'Instead of...'

'BALLOON' GLASS

Cognac
Armagnac
Marc
Whisky
Calvados
Slivovitz
Kirsch
Other eaux de vie

'VERRE CHEMINÉE'

Cognac
Armagnac
Marc
Eaux de vie

BITTERGLASS

Jenever
Vodka
Bitters such as Underberg

LIQUEURGLASS

Bénédictine
Crème de menthe
Grand Marnier
Cointreau
Cherry Brandy
Curacao
Other liqueurs

COCKTAILGLASS

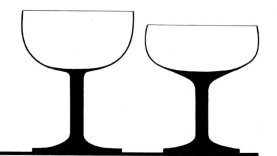

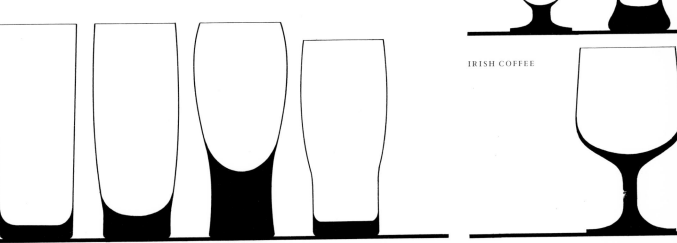

WHISKY GLASS
Whisky
Whisky on the rocks
Cocktails

WHISKY-AND-SODA GLASS

**SLIVOVITZ
VODKA**

LONG DRINK GLASS
Gin-and-tonic
Vodka in long drinks
Ouzo
Rum in long drinks

**PERNOD
RICARD**

IRISH COFFEE

Glossary

Alcohol
Arabic-derived word for an organic compound. The alcohol in our spirits and liqueurs is ethyl alcohol or ethanol, a colourless liquid formed by fermentation by yeast of sugary substances such as fruit, sugar-cane, honey etc., or starchy substances, such as wheat, rice or potatoes.

Alcool blanc
French term for a colourless, dry distillation, either from the fermented mash of fruit or from fruit steeped in alcohol and then re-distilled.

Alembic
Arabic word for a simple pot still. Alembics are still in use for the distillation of cognac and armagnac.

Apéritif
French word for a drink taken before a meal to stimulate the appetite.

Aqua Vitae
Literally 'Water of Life', this Latin name for all spirits can be found in the Scandinavian 'aquavit', and the French 'eau de vie'.

Bitters
Spirits flavoured with herbs, generally of a medicinal nature, usually drunk diluted as an apéritif or digestif or as a flavouring in mixed drinks.

Blend
A mixture of different malt and grain whiskies, usually the product of several distilleries.

Boisé
The infusion of oak-chips in a brandy, to hasten the process of mellowing and maturing.

Caramel
Burnt sugar sometimes added to brandies to deepen the colour of commercial brands and to keep colour consistent.

Coffey, Aeneas
Inspector-General of Irish Excise. Patented in 1830 or 1833 the Coffey still or patent still for the continuous distillation of spirits.

Congenerics
Impurities remaining in the distilled product during the ageing of spirits in wood and contributing to the characteristic flavour of the finished product.

Cordial
American name for sweetened and flavoured liqueurs.

Crème
Extra sweetened liqueur with a sugar content of forty percent.

Diastase
Enzyme produced by the germination of grains, converting starch into sugar.

Digestif
French word for a sweet after-dinner drink. Originally a herbal liqueur or bitters taken before or after a meal to aid digestion.

Distillation
The process of turning a liquid into vapour by heating it, then bringing it back to liquid form by condensation, in the course of which drops trickle down.

Dunder
Solid matter left in the still after the distillation of rum.

Eau de vie
French for 'Water of Life', generally used for the dry, colourless spirits distilled from fruit.

Elixir
Herb-flavoured liqueurs, originally produced by alchemists in their attics or monks in their monasteries as magic potions and as medicines.

Faible
Mixture of cognac and distilled water.

Grain whisky
Whisky distilled in patent stills from maize (corn) or grain.

Liqueur
Alcohol-based drink flavoured with herbs, seeds or fruits, from the Latin word 'liquor'.

Maceration
Process of steeping herbs or fruits in a cold spirit, to give it an aromatic flavour.

Malt whisky
Whisky distilled in pot stills from malted grain, usually barley.

Mash
Grain which has been steeped in hot water to moisten the starch.

Patent still
Coffey still or continuous still. In this still the alcohol is rectified as it is being separated from the water in whatever the original fermented liquid may be, thus producing a strong, comparatively pure, or neutral spirit.

Percentage
Measure to define the alcoholic content of spirits and liqueurs, stated in terms of degrees Gay-Lussac. This can be a percentage of volume or of weight.

Percolation
Process whereby a hot or cold spirit is trickled or forced through an aromatic substance of herbs or fruits to give the spirit an aromatic flavour.

Pot still
In this still the alcohol is distilled in two separate, non-continuous kettles, whereby much of the character of the liquid is retained. Cognac and malt whisky are always distilled in pot stills.

Proof
Measure to define the alcoholic content of spirits and liqueurs. 'Proof' in the USA is twice the alcohol percentage by volume. In Britain the *Sikes* system is fixed as to that 100 British proof equals 57,1 percent ethyl alcohol by volume.

Sikes, Bartholomew
Devised in 1816 in Britain a method of determination of alcoholic content. This Sikes 'proof' is still in use in Great Britain.

Stein, Robert
Invented in 1826 a continuous still for the rapid distillation of grain spirits. Later a similar device was patented by Aeneas Coffey, hence the name Coffey still.

Still
see Patent still and Pot still.

Uisge Beatha
Gaelic name for 'Water of Life' from which 'whisky' has been derived.

VSOP
Very Superior Old Pale. A Cognac which must be at least four years old, in practice usually older.

XO
Extra Old. Definition on labels for a matured product.

Abricot, Eau de vie d' –
see Eau de vie d'abricot

Abricotine
Sweet cordial based on apricots

Absinthe
Aperitif based on spirit but named after
one of its informing herbs – wormwood.
Outlawed in France and elsewhere – but
not in Spain. Its near relative is *pastis*, 72

Advocaat
Rich, sweet, thick cordial made of egg
yolks, sugar and neutral spirit

Aguardiente
A generic name for spirits in Portugal
and more particularly for grape
brandy, 37

Aiguebelle
Sweet herb-flavoured liqueur from the
South of France. As with *Chartreuse* there
are a green and a yellow version and a
monastic pedigree

Akvavit
see *aquavit*

Alsace, Eau de vie d' –
see Eau de vie d'Alsace

Alsace, Kirsch d' –
see Kirsch d'Alsace

Amaretto
Sweet nutty-flavoured Italian liqueur
based on spirit and the kernels of apricot
stones. There are various brands, some
known as *amaro*

Amaro
see *Amaretto*

American Whiskey
see under *Whiskey*

Amer picon
Proprietary French bitters, usually taken
diluted, as an aperitif, 105

Angelique
Herbal liqueur from the Pyrenees based
on angelica root

Angostura
Proprietary tonic bitters from Trinidad,
so strong and bitter that it cannot be taken
neat, but is added by the drop to give
flavour and colour to other drinks, 58, 105

Anisette
Sweet, anis-flavoured after-dinner
liqueur. There are many brands, 23, 24

Anvers, Elixir d' –
see Elixir d'Anvers

Applejack
American equivalent of the French
Calvados. A dry, colourless spirit made
from apples by way of distilled
cider or eau de vie de cidre, 85

Apricot brandy
Virtually all liqueur firms have their own
brand of this sweet liqueur based on
brandy or other spirit and flavoured with
apricots, and usually their stones,
85, 86, 111

Apricotine
see *Abricotine*

Aquavit
The traditional spirit of the Scandinavian
countries; colourless, distilled from grain,
and usually flavoured with carraway, but
there are many varieties in flavouring.
Drunk neat and ice-cold.
Also spelled *akvavit*, especially in
Denmark, 69–70, 76

Armagnac
The second of France's two great
brandies, not so widely known as *Cognac*,
nor so subtle, but admired by many for
its robust raciness of the soil. From a
strictly delimited area in South-west
France and matured in the dark-veined
oak of the region, 27, 29, 31, 32, 33, 36,
76, 85, 97

Armorique, Elixir d' –
see Elixir d'Armorique

Arrack
Potent spirit distilled in South-East Asia from palm-sap, or rice or sugar cane, 70, 71, 75

Asbach Uralt
Proprietary grape brandy made in Germany from imported wines – French, Italian and Yugoslav. Made in much the same way as *Cognac*, 37

Aurum
Sweet, golden Italian proprietary liqueur, orange-flavoured, 109

B-and-B
At one time, there were those who asked the barman or the wine-waiter to mix a *Bénédictine* half-and-half with brandy, thus creating a Bénédictine-and-brandy, that cut the sweetness but preserved the flavour of Bénédictine neat. Then the Bénédictine firm took to producing B-and-B ready mixed, under its own label, 98

Bagaceiro
Portuguese eau de vie made from pips and stalks of grapes after wine-making

Baie de houx, Eau de vie de –
see Eau de vie de baie de houx

Bailey's Irish Cream
see Irish Cream

Bananes, Crème de –
see Crème de bananes

Barack Palinka
Dry, colourless eau de vie of apricots and their kernels. Others exist, but under this name the Hungarian product is the most famous, 86

Barenfang
see *Barenjäger*

Barenjäger
Sweet liqueur, with honey, from East Prussia

Basler Kirschwasser
see *Kirschwasser*

Battleaxe
A proprietary Italian rum liqueur, 100

Bénédictine D.O.M.
Renowned French proprietary liqueur, sweet, herb-flavoured and based on brandy, 18, 19, 97, 98, 115

Bessenjenever
Dutch medium-sweet black currant cordial based on dry gin or neutral spirit, 60

Blackberry Brandy
Can be applied either to the dry colourless eau de vie distilled from blackberries or to a sweet cordial based on brandy and blackberry flavoured

Boonekamp
Strong, aromatic digestive bitters, originally Dutch, now German

Bourbon
Classic American *whiskey*, named after Bourbon county in Kentucky. Distilled from a mash mostly of corn (maize), 52, 53, 111, 112

Brandy
Derived from the Dutch word *brandewijn*, meaning 'burned wine'.
Originally 'distilled grape juice', but there are now dry, colourless spirits distilled from fruits and sweet fruit-flavoured cordials, to both of which the word brandy is applied, 27–40, 85, 87, 102, 104, 107, 110, 111

Brandy, Apricot –
see Apricot brandy

Brandy, Blackberry –
see Blackberry brandy

Brandy, Cherry –
see Cherry brandy

Brandy, Orange –
see Orange brandy

Cacao, Crème de –
see Crème de cacao

Café, Crème de –
see Crème de café

Calvados
Eau de vie distilled from cider from the French apple-growing district of Calvados in Normandy, 86, 88, 89, 91

Campari
Bitter sweet Italian aperitif, taken with vermouth in cocktails or soda water, 105

Canadian Whisky
see under *Whisky*

Cassis, Crème de –
see Crème de cassis

Centerbe
Sweet Italian liqueur said to be compounded from a hundred herbs – hence the name, 97

Cerises, Eau de vie de –
see Eau de vie de cerises

Chartreuse
One of the – perhaps the – best known of all proprietary liqueurs; based on a number of herbs, sweet and pungent. The green Chartreuse is stronger and more expensive than the yellow, 23, 24, 93, 94, 95, 97, 102, 112

Cherry brandy
Sweet cordial or liqueur made sometimes from bitter, sometimes from sweet cherries, sometimes from cherries with their crushed stones according to the formula of the house producing it, and sometimes based on brandy, sometimes on neutral spirit, 85, 107, 109, 110, 111

Cherry Whisky
As *Cherry brandy*, but with a whisky base, and much less widely made and distributed, 111

Chocolate Liqueur, Royal Mint –
see Royal Mint Chocolate Liqueur

Cidre, Eau de vie de –
see Eau de vie de cidre

Citroenjenever
Dutch medium-sweet lemon cordial based on dry gin or neutral spirit, 60

Coffee Liqueur, Irish –
see Irish Coffee Liqueur

Coffee Liqueur, Old Vienna –
see Old Vienna Coffee Liqueur

Cognac
The world's most famous grape brandy, made only in one strictly delimited region of South-western France, by equally strictly defined processes, 27, 29, 31, 32, 33, 34, 35, 36, 47, 55, 76, 82, 85, 89, 91, 97, 115

Cointreau
Proprietary sweet, colourless orange-flavoured liqueur, 109

Cordial Médoc
Sweet French proprietary liqueur from Medoc, the claret country, based on brandy and flavoured with both fruits and herbs, 97

Cream, Bailey's Irish
see Irish Cream

Crème
Extra sweetened liqueur

Crème de bananes
Sweet liqueur, banana-flavoured

Crème de cacao
Sweet liqueur, cocoa- or chocolate-flavoured, 115

Crème de café
Sweet liqueur, coffee-flavoured

Crème de cassis
Rich black currant cordial, much used in France as an additive to vermouth, champagne or white wine: 'vermouth-cassis', 'champagne-cassis' and 'vin blanc-cassis' – this last often referred to as 'rince-cochon' or 'Kir', 112, 113

Crème de fraises
Sweet liqueur, strawberry-flavoured

Crème de framboises
Sweet liqueur, raspberry-flavoured

Crème de kirsch
Sweet liqueur, cherry-flavoured. See also under *Cherry brandy*. Not to be confused with the dry eau de vie, usually referred to as *Kirsch*

Crème de menthe
Bright green or colourless peppermint flavoured sweet liqueur usually drunk, unlike other liqueurs, 'frappé' (on crushed ice) and through a straw. There are many brands, 103

Crème de mocca
see Crème de café

Crème de noisette
Hazelnut flavoured sweet liqueur

Crème de noyaux
Sweet liqueur flavoured with hazelnuts or other nuts or the kernels of fruit stones or a combination of such, 111

Crème de prunelles
Sweet liqueur flavoured with sloes, similar to English *Sloe gin*

Crème de roses
Sweet liqueur flavoured with rose-essence

Crème de thé
Tea-flavoured sweet liqueur, rarely to be found

Crème de vanille
Vanilla-flavoured sweet liqueur

Crème de violette
Violet-coloured, violet-scented and violet-flavoured sweet liqueur

Cuarenta y tres
Spanish sweet liqueur, so called because it was the fourty-third attempt that succeeded in producing this herb-flavoured liqueur, 102

Cumquat
Sweet citrus-flavoured liqueur made in Corfu from the locally grown miniature Japanese orange of the same name, 109

Curaçao
Generic name for sweet orange-flavoured liqueurs of which there are many proprietary brands differing in colour and style, some based on brandy, some on neutral spirit. Named after the Dutch West-Indian island from the bitter oranges of which the liqueur was made. See also *Triple Sec Curaçao*, 23, 107, 109

Cynar
Bitter-sweet Italian proprietary drink based on artichokes, taken neat as a digestive or diluted as an aperitif, 105

Danziger Goldwasser
Sweet kummel-type liqueur flavoured with carraway and aniseed, colourless but with flecks of gold leaf afloat in it, 104

Demerara Rum
Traditionally one of the darker, thicker and more pungent of the West-Indian rums, though nowadays Demerara also produces lighter and drier rums, 79

Drambuie
Proprietary sweet Scottish liqueur based on whisky, herbs and honey, 99, 102, 103, 112

Dry Gin
see under *Gin*

127

Eau de vie

Strictly speaking any distillation is an eau de vie. *Cognac* for instance is an eau de vie de vin, *Calvados* an eau de vie de cidre. But in general usage the term is applied almost exclusively to the dry, colourless distillations from fruits – termed by the French 'alcools blancs'

Eau de vie d'abricote

Dry, colourless spirit distilled from apricots

Eau de vie d'Alsace

see *Eau de vie de fruits d'Alsace*

Eau de vie de baie de houx

Dry, colourless spirit distilled from holly-berries. Very rare, 90

Eau de vie de cerises

Dry distillation from cherries. See also *Eau de vie de kirsch*

Eau de vie de cidre

Dry colourless spirit, distilled from cider. *Calvados* is the best known

Eau de vie de figues

Dry distillation from figs. Rare

Eau de vie de framboises

Dry distillation at one time from wild, but now from cultivated raspberries – still one of the most sought after and expensive of the eaux de vie, 85, 87, 91

Eau de vie de fruits d'Alsace

An undistinguished distillation from mixed fruits as made in Alsace, when there is not enough of any one fruit for an eau de vie to be made from it, 91

Eau de vie de kirsch

Dry distillation from sour black cherries – much used to enhance a flavour of fresh fruit and fresh fruit salads, 86, 87, 88, 91, 107

Eau de vie de marc

see under *Marc*

Eau de vie de mirabelles

Dry distillation from the very small sweet golden plum, 91

Eau de vie de poires

Dry distillation from pears, sometimes known as *Poire Williams, Williamine* or *Williamsbirne*, 91

Eau de vie de pommes

see *Eau de vie de cidre* and *Calvados*

Eau de vie de quetsch

Dry distillation from the small sour, purple 'switzen' plum, 91

Elixir d'Anvers

Belgian bitter-sweet liqueur, flavoured with herbs and seeds and yellow in colour, though the same firm now produces the green Elixir de Spa

Elixir d'Armorique

Bitter-sweet herbal liqueur from Launion in Normandy

Elixir de Monbazillac

Herbal liqueur from the southern part of France

Elixir de Mondorf

Digestive liqueur from Luxembourg, somewhat similar to *Elixer de Spa*

Elixir de Spa

Sweet Belgian green liqueur based on plants and herbs and claiming digestive properties, 95

Elixir végétal

Highly concentrated essence of *green Chartreuse*, too strong to be drunk except as drops in water or on sugar, as a digestive, 93

Ettaler

Sweet German herb-based liqueur, somewhat similar in style to *Chartreuse* – there are green and yellow versions – made at a monastery near Oberammergau in the Bavarian Alps, 95

Fernet branca
Italian aromatic bitters, taken with soda
as an aperitif or as a digestive, 105

Figues, Eau de vie de –
see Eau de vie de Figues

Fior d'Alpi
Sweet Italian herb liqueur, 101

Fleur des Alpes
Sweet French herb liqueur, 101

Forbidden fruit
American liqueur, sweet with an
undertone of bitterness, based on citrus
fruits, 25, 109

Fraises, Crème de –
see Crème de fraises

Fraises de bois, Liqueur de –
see Liqueur de fraises de bois

Framboise
The French word for raspberry. Usually
applied, *tout court*, to the dry eau de vie
de framboise 85, 87, 91

Framboise sauvage
Applied to the eau de vie from the wild
raspberries of Alsace and the nearby
regions. Distilled less and less frequently,
these days, because of the expense of
finding and picking them

Framboises, Crème de –
see Crème de framboises

Framboises, Eau de vie de –
see Eau de vie de framboises

Framboises, Liqueur de –
see Liqueur de framboises

Fundador
Proprietary name for Spanish brandy, 37

Galliano
Italian sweet flavoured herb liqueur,
100, 101

Genever
see *Jenever*

Gin
Generally speaking, a neutral or
near-neutral spirit flavoured with juniper
berries and other 'botanicals'. But there
are different styles, both of making and
of taking, see *London Gin, Plymouth Gin,
Jenever* and *Steinhäger,* 55–63, 76

Ginger Liqueur
Richly sweet liqueur flavoured with
ginger. Not widely known, 103

Glayva
Sweet liqueur made in Scotland from
whisky and herbs, 103

Glen Mist
Whisky-based sweet liqueur, similar to
Glayva, 103

Goldwasser, Danziger –
see Danziger Goldwasser

Grand Marnier
Justifiably famous, rich, sweet French
proprietary liqueur, based on distillation
of oranges steeped in *Cognac.* Much used
in the cooking of elaborate confections as
well as drunk after dinner as a liqueur,
109, 115

Grappa
Distilled in Italy and California from the
residue of the skins, pips and stalks of
grapes after they have been pressed for
wine making. The equivalent of the
French *Marc;* a strong, earthy, colourless
dry spirit, 36, 39

Grappa alla ruta
Grappa, slightly flavoured and faintly
coloured by the addition of a grass-like
herb, 36

Grignan
Strong sweet herb liqueur made by
monks in the Rhône valley. Not very well
known, 95

Half om half
Bitter-sweet Dutch liqueur consisting of
half and half *Curaçao* and orange bitters,
107

Himbeergeist
Dry, colourless eau de vie distilled in
Germany from alcohol in which
raspberries have been macerated. The
equivalent of the French *Eau de vie de
framboises*, 85

Houx, Eau de vie de baie de –
see Eau de vie de baie de houx

Hum, van der
see Van der Hum

Irish Coffee Liqueur
Sweet and rich liqueur, made in Ireland
of whiskey, honey, herbs, and coffee
essence. Also known as *Irish velvet*, 116

Irish Cream
A rich blend of chocolate cream and Irish
whiskey. Also known under brand name
as *Bailey's Irish Cream*, 115

Irish Mist
Sweet liqueur made in Ireland from
whiskey and herbs, 99, 103, 116

Irish Velvet
see *Irish Coffee Liqueur*

Irish Whiskey
see under *Whiskey*

Izarra
Herb-flavoured liqueur from the Basque
part of the French Pyrenees, 97

Jägermeister
Sweet German herb-flavoured liqueur,
103

Jamaica Rum
Traditionally one of the darker, richer and
more aromatic of West-Indian rums, but
as in *Demerara*, lighter rums are also now
being produced, 79

Jenever
Dutch gin, sometimes spelled *genever* and
sometimes known abroad as 'Hollands'.
More pungent than London gin and,
unlike London gin, unvariably drunk
neat. 'Jonge' (young) jenever is lighter
and drier than 'oude' (old), 55–60

Jonge jenever
see under *Jenever*

Kahlua
Proprietary sweet coffee-based Mexican
liqueur, also made under licence in
Denmark, 115, 116

Kanyak
Generic Turkish name for local grape
brandies, 37

Karpi
Fragrant, bitter-sweet Finnish liqueur
flavoured with cranberries and other
sub-Arctic fruit, 112

Kirsch
Generic name for *Eau de vie de cerises*
(France) or *Kirschwasser* (German and
Swiss). *Kirsch d'Alsace* is best known, 85,
86, 87, 88, 91, 107

Kirsch, Crème de –
see Crème de kirsch

Kirschwasser
German and Swiss name for *Eau de vie
de cerises*. Best known are Schwarzwalder
Kirschwasser from the German Black
Forest and *Basler Kirschwasser* from
Switzerland, 85, 86, 87, 88, 107

Kitro
Greek citrus-flavoured sweet liqueur, 109

Kloster Bitter
German name for bitters, originally made
in monasteries, now being produced
under different brand names

Koum Kouat
see *Cumquat*

130

Kummel
There are many proprietary brands of this sweet carraway-flavoured colourless liqueur, most of them from North-European countries. Has recognised digestive properties, 104

Lakka
Bitter-sweet Finnish liqueur based on cloudberries, 112

Latte di Suocera
'Mother-in-Law's Milk' – a proprietary Italian sweet herb-flavoured liqueur, 100

Linie Aquavit
Norwegian brand of *aquavit* so named because it crosses the 'Line' (the Equator) in casks in cargo ships, thus acquiring a pale golden colour and an added mellowness, 70

Liqueur de framboise
Sweet liqueur with raspberry flavour

Liqueur de fraises de bois
Sweet liqueur flavoured with wild strawberries

London gin
The driest of gins, made by flavouring a virtually neutral spirit, distilled from grain. Used almost always as a basis for mixed drinks, 58, 59, 60, 61, 63

Malt Whisky
Scotch whisky, made of malted barley and distilled in pot stills, mostly blended with other malt or grain whiskies, 45–52

Mandarine
Sweet liqueur with the flavour of the small tangerine-type orange mandarin. Good brands come from French, Belgian and Danish firms, 109

Maraschino
Originally made in Dalmatia (now part of Yugoslavia) from local bitter-sweet cherries, this sweet colourless liqueur is now made by many manufacturers, 109

Marc
More correctly *Eau de vie de marc*, the earthy tasting, dry, usually colourless spirit distilled from the residue of skins, pips and stalks left after grapes have been pressed for wine-making. See also *Grappa*, 36, 39, 76

Marc de Bourgogne
Eau de vie de marc from the Burgundy district, 36

Marc de Champagne
Eau de vie de marc from the Champagne district, 36

Marc de Gewurztraminer
An Alsatian eau de vie de marc distilled from the Gewurztraminer grape, 36

Marc de Meursault
Eau de vie de marc from Meursault, 36

Marc de Sancerre
Eau de vie de marc from Sancerre

Marillenbrand
Austrian dry, colourless distillation from apricots

Mastika
Resinated Greek grape-brandy, 37

Menthe, Crème de
see Crème de menthe

Mentuccia
Another name for the Italian *Centerbe*, 97

Mescal
Mexican spirit distilled from a particular type of cactus from which the drug mescalin also derives. *Tequila* is a variety from a specially defined district, 85

Mesimarja
Sweet Finnish blackberry liqueur, 112

Metaxa
Well-known Greek brandy produced by the firm of the same name

Millefiori
Italian sweet herb liqueur, said to contain the essence of 'a thousand flowers', hence the name, 101

Mint Liqueur
Virtually all liqueur producing firms make sweet after-dinner mint-flavoured liqueurs, under various names. See also *Crème de menthe*

Mirabelle, Eau de vie de –
see Eau de vie de mirabelle

Mocca, Crème de –
see Crème de mocca

Monbazillac, Elixir de –
see Elixir de Monbazillac

Mondorf, Elixir de –
see Elixir de Mondorf

Mûre
Eau de vie of blackberries, 91

Myrtille
Eau de vie of bilberries, 91

Noisette, Crème de –
see Crème de noisette

Noyaux, Crème de –
see Crème de noyaux

Obstwasser
Undistinguished distillation from mixed fruits as made in Germany, mainly in the Black Forest

Old Vienna Coffee Liqueur
Proprietary sweet liqueur made in Vienna of coffee essence and French brandy, 116

Orange brandy
Sweet orange-flavoured liqueur of which many brands are made 24

Oranjebitter
Aromatic, orange-flavoured bitters, to be served neat

Oude jenever
see under *Jenever*

Ouzo
Greek aperitif with brandy or neutral spirit base, flavoured with aniseed. Colourless until water is added, when it becomes opalescent, 37, 71

Parfait amour
Very sweet liqueur, coloured, flavoured and scented to seem to be a luscious essence of violets. Made by various Dutch and French firms, 25, 109

Pastis
Generic name for the French aperitif that is closely related to the now forbidden *absinth*. A colourless spirit flavoured with aniseed that becomes opalescent when water is added. Best known brands are *Pernod* and *Ricard*. See also *Ouzo*, 72

Pêche
Sweet peach-flavoured liqueur, 111

Pelinkovac
Bitter-sweet dark-coloured liqueur based on herbs and red wine, of Yugoslav origin but now made in Italy, 100

Peppermint Liqueur
There are many brands, some green, some colourless, of this sweet after-dinner liqueur, strongly flavoured with peppermint, 103

Pernod
see *pastis*

Persico
Sweet peach-flavoured liqueur made from almonds

Pimm's no. 1 Cup
A proprietary concentrate of gin, aromatics and sweetening to which sparkling bottled lemonade is added. If instead of lemonade sweet champagne is added the drink is called 'Pimm's Royal', 58

Pimpeltjens
Proprietary sweet Dutch liqueur based partly on herbs, partly on the peel of sweet and bitter oranges, 108

Pineau des Charentes
Sweet aperitif made by adding cognac to grape juice and thus checking fermentation

Pisco
Generic name for brandy in Latin-American countries, whether distilled from grape juice or, like *Marc* and *Grappa*, from the solids left after grapes have been pressed for wine-making, 37

Plymouth Gin
Made in the same way as *London gin* but somewhat more pungently flavoured – between London gin and *Jenever* in style, 58, 59

Poires, Eau de vie de –
see Eau de vie de poires

Poire Williams
see Eau de vie de poires

Pommes, Eau de vie de –
see Eau de vie de pommes

Portakal
Sweet Turkish citrus-flavoured liqueur, 109

Prunelle
Dry, colourless eau de vie distilled from sloes, 91

Prunelles, Crème de –
see Crème de prunelles

Punsch
Spicy cordial, made in Sweden but based on imported Batavian *Arrack*, taken neat as a liqueur or with hot water as a punch, 71

Quetsch, Eau de vie de –
see Eau de vie de quetsch

Raki
A general name in the Near East for almost any sort of distilled spirit, 71

Raspail
Now a proprietary sweet liqueur – yellow and herb-based – but named after a mid-nineteenth century Frenchman, François Raspail, said to have been a precursor of Pasteur, who devised what he held to be a digestive formula

Ratafia
General term for sweet aperitifs made by adding brandy or other spirits to fresh grape juice to prevent fermentation and the conversion of the fruit sugar to alcohol. Usually sold with a regional name, as *Ratafia de Champagne*. Another example is *Pineau des Charentes*

Rhum
see *Rum*

Rhum Barbancourt
A delicate liqueur rum from Haiti, 82

Rhum Negrita
A standard-type rum imported by the Bordeaux firm of Bardinet and much used in French kitchens, 81

Rhum Saint James
Rich aromatic rum from Martinique, 81

Ricard
Proprietary brand name of *pastis*, 72

Roses, Crème de –
see Crème de roses

Royal Mint Chocolate Liqueur
Proprietary sweet liqueur combining mint and chocolate flavours, 115

Rum
The spirit of sugar-cane, produced in various ways and in various types, mostly in the Caribbean. See also *Demerara rum*, *Jamaica rum*, *Rhum Barbancourt*, *Rhum Negrita*, *Rhum Saint James*, 75–83

Rye
One of the two classic North-American whiskeys, distilled chiefly from rye, the other being *Bourbon*, distilled from corn, 52, 53, 112

Sabra
Red, bitter-sweet Israeli liqueur flavoured with the fruit of the sabra cactus

Sake
The name given in Japan both to a wine made from fermented rice and to the spirit distilled from it, 70

Sambuca
Sweet Italian proprietary liqueur, colourless and flavoured with an anise-like herb, 103

Schinkenhäger
Proprietary name for a German gin, 56

Scotch Whisky
see under *Whisky*

Schwarzwalder Kirschwasser
see under *Kirschwasser*

Sechsämter Tropfen
German bitter-sweet herb liqueur

Sénancole, la
Sweet liqueur, similar to yellow *Chartreuse*, made by Cistercians of the Abby of Sénanque, in the South of France, 95

Sève Patricia
Proprietary brand of Sève, a sweet herb-flavoured liqueur, 115

Slivovitz
Best known of the Balkan and Eastern-Adriatic-coast dry colourless eaux de vie, distilled from plums, 86, 88, 91

Sloe Gin
Sweet rich English liqueur made by steeping ripe sloes in sweetened gin. Also made in other countries, 111

Sorbes
Dry, colourless eau de vie of rowan-berries, 91

Southern Comfort
Proprietary, sweet but full-flavoured American liqueur with a base of old Bourbon whiskey flavoured with peaches, oranges and herbs, 111, 112

Spa, Elixir de –
see Elixir de Spa

Steinhäger
German gin, particularly aromatic because made, not by flavouring a more or less neutral spirit, but by distilling from fermented juniper berries, 56

Stonsdorfer
German aromatic bitters, 105

Strega
Sweet, herb-flavoured greeny-gold liqueur from Southern Italy, 99, 100

Suze à la Gentiane
Strongly flavoured proprietary French aperitif, based on gentian root and taken diluted. Said to have digestive properties

Tequila
Mexican spirit distilled from a variety of agave or cactus, see also *Mescal*, 85, 86

Thé, Crème de –
see Crème de thé

Tia Maria
Proprietary liqueur based on Jamaican rum and essence of Jamaican coffee, 116

Trappistine
Herb-flavoured French liqueur made from a Trappist monastery's formula, 95

Tresterschnapps
German eau de vie made from the skins, stalks and pips of grapes after they have been pressed for wine. The equivalent of *Marc* and *Grappa*, 36

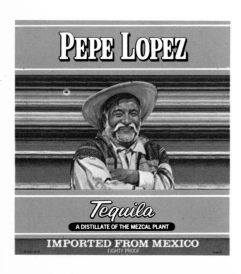

Triple Sec Curaçao
Many brands of orange-flavoured liqueur claim to be trebly dry. *Cointreau* is the best-known, but all in fact are sweet. See also *Curaçao*, 107, 109

Underberg
Strong aromatic German digestive bitters to be taken only in small doses, and medicinally, 105

Van der Hum
Sweet South African liqueur flavoured with the native tangerine-like Naartjes. A generic name, though *Bertram's* is the best-known proprietary brand, 108

Vanille, Crème de –
see Crème de vanille

Végétal, Elixir –
see Elixir Végétal

Verveine du Velay
French proprietary brandy-based herb-flavoured liqueur, green and yellow, like *Chartreuse*, but with more bitter, verveine flavour

Vieille cure
Herb liqueur based on a blend of *Cognac* and *Armagnac*, 97

Vienna Coffee Liqueur, Old –
see Old Vienna Coffee Liqueur

Violette, Crème de –
see Crème de violette

Vodka
The traditional dry schnapps or aquavit of the Slav countries and of Finland, distilled usually from wheat but sometimes from corn or rye. Usually drunk neat, ice-cold as an almost neutral spirit, but there are flavoured vodkas, especially from Poland.
Now vodka is produced also in Western Europe and especially in the United States, where it is very popular, 63, 69, 76

Wacholder
German distillation of grain or neutral alcohol to which a distillation of juniper berries has been added. See also *Steinhäger* and *Schinkenhäger*

Wasser
German name for *eau de vie*

Whiskey, American –
Note the spelling. The classic American whiskeys are *Bourbon*, distilled from a mash largely of corn (maize) and *Rye*, from a rye mash. But there are blends and variants 43, 52

Whiskey, Irish –
Note the spelling. Like Scotch, a blend of malt and grain whiskeys, but still with a marked malty flavour, 43, 51, 52, 53

Whisky, Canadian –
Note the spelling. From a blend of grains and more like Rye than Bourbon, more like Irish than Scotch, but lighter then any of them, 53

Whisky, Cherry –
see Cherry whisky

Whisky, Scotch –
Note the spelling. 'Scotch whisky', so called, is a blend of neutral grain whisky from patent stills and flavoury malt whisky from old-fashioned pot stills, but the latter is obtainable unblended as 'Highland malt' or 'straight malt', 43–53 See also malt whisky

Williamine
see Eau de vie de poire

Williamsbirne
see Eau de vie de poire

Williams, Poire –
see Poire Williams

Zwetschgenwasser
Dry, colourless distillation from plums from the Black Forest

Firms and brand-names mentioned in the text

Alcoholic Strength

In most parts of the world the alcohol-content of spirits is expressed as a percentage, by degrees Gay Lussac. This is a percentage of volume or of weight.

In the United States and the United Kingdom the term 'proof' is used. The two countries determine proof differently. Alcoholic proof in the United Kingdom is fixed so that 100 % British proof (or Sikes) equals 57,14 % ethyl alcohol by volume. In the American system 'proof' is twice the alcohol content by volume. A spirit labeled 40 % will be 80 proof in the United States and 70 proof in the United Kingdom.

% Gay Lussac	American Proof	British (or Sikes) Proof
10	20	17,50
20	40	35
30	60	52,50
40	80	70
41	82	71,75
42	84	73,50
43	86	75,25
44	88	77
45	90	78,75
50	100	87,50
57,14	114.28	100
60	120	105

BOTTLE SIZES

1,87 dl (0,187 l) =	6.32 fl. oz. US =	6.58 fl. oz. British
3,75 dl (0,375 l) =	12.68 fl. oz. US =	13.20 fl. oz. British
7 dl (0,7 l) =	23.67 fl. oz. US =	24.64 fl. oz. British
7,5 dl (0,75 l) =	25.36 fl. oz. US =	26.40 fl. oz. British
1 l =	33.81 fl. oz. US =	35.20 fl. oz. British

LIQUID MEASURES

1 fl. oz. British	=	28.4 ml metric =	.96 fl. oz. US
1 imp. pint British	=	5.68 dl metric =	1 pt 3.22 fl. oz. US
1 imp. quart British	=	1.14 l metric =	1 qt 6.43 fl. oz. US
1 imp. gal. British	=	4.56 l metric =	1 gal. 25.6 fl. oz. US
1 fl. oz. US	=	29.6 ml metric =	1.04 fl. oz. British
1 pt US	=	4.73 dl metric =	16.65 fl. oz. British
			.833 imp. gallon British
1 qt US	=	3.79 l metric =	1 imp. pt 13.31 fl. oz. British

Sources of illustrations

Photographs by Ed Suister: 6–7, 8, 16, 22, 24, 26, 28, 30, 33, 34, 36, 39, 41, 42, 53, 54, 56, 59, 65, 66, 69, 72, 74, 82, 83, 84, 86, 87, 90, 92, 95, 99, 101, 103, 104–105, 106, 108, 109, 114, 116

ACKNOWLEDGEMENTS FOR ILLUSTRATIONS

The Glenlivet Distillers 11, 12, 18
Frans Hals Museum, Haarlem 13
Marie Brizard France s.a., Bordeaux 14
Bibliotheek van de Teylers Stichting, Haarlem 18, 19, 23, 56, 71, 87, 89, 100, 110
Fa. P. Melchers, Schiedam 24, 57, 65
Bureau National du Cognac 29, 31
Germanisches Nationalmuseum, Nürnberg 37
Michael Broadbent Esq. 40
J & B Ltd., from Rare Images/A view of J & B, Photo Art Kane 44
The Scottish Tourist Board 45
John Bartholomew & Son Ltd., Edinburgh 46
The Scotch Whisky Association 48–49
The Glenlivet Distillers, Photo Bryan and Shear Ltd. 50
Irish Distillers Ltd. 51
nv Koninklijke Distilleerderijen Erven Lucas Bols, Nieuw Vennep 56, 117
Nationaal Gedistilleerd Museum, Schiedam 57
Henkes Verenigde Distilleerderijen, Hendrik Ido Ambacht 60
Condé Nast Publications Ltd. 61
Gilbey Vintners Ltd., London 64
Ets. Pernod, Paris 73
British Museum, London 76
Radio Times Hulton Picture Library 77
H.H. Pott Nfgr, Flensburg 78–79, 80
National Maritime Museum, Greenwich 81
Photostudio Heinz Preisig, Sion 91
Chartreuse Diffusion s.a., Voiron 94
Bénédictine s.a., Fécamp 98
Ognibeni & Co. b.v., Amsterdam 105
British Tourist Office, London 110
Charles Kinloch & Co. Ltd., London 112
Snark International, London 113

Daiches, David, *Scotch Whisky*, London 1969

Doxat, John, *Drinks and drinking*, London 1971

Hallgarten, Peter, *Liqueurs*, London 1967

Hannum and Blumberg, *Brandies and Liqueurs of the World*, New York, 1976

Lichine, Alexis, *Encyclopaedia of Wines and Spirits*, 3rd, (revised) edition, New York, 1974

Marrison, L.W., *Wines and Spirits*, revised edition, London, 1963

McGuire, E.B., *Irish Whiskey*, Dublin, 1973

Ray, Cyril, *Cognac*, London, 1973